THE BEER BANDIT CAPER

THE MOUNTIES, THEIR MAN AND MEXICO'S MISSING MOOSEHEAD

HARVEY SAWLER

NIMBUS
PUBLISHING

Nimbus Publishing Limited
PO Box 9166
Halifax, NS B3K 5M8
(902) 455-4286

Printed and bound in Canada

Design: Margaret Issenman, MGDC
Front cover: Hudson Design Group, Moncton, New Brunswick
Author photo: Stephen MacGillivray

Library and Archives Canada Cataloguing in Publication

Sawler, Harvey, 1954-
The beer bandit caper : the Mounties, their man and Mexico's missing Moosehead / Harvey Sawler.

ISBN 1-55109-546-7

1. Cargo theft—New Brunswick. 2. Haines, Wade. 3. Moosehead Breweries. 4. Criminal investigation—New Brunswick. I. Title.

HV6665.C32 2004 S29 2005   364.16'2'097151   C2005-904383-0

We acknowledge the financial support of the Government of Canada through the Book Publishing Industry Development Program (BPIDP) and the Canada Council, and of the Province of Nova Scotia through the Department of Tourism, Culture and Heritage for our publishing activities.

Wade Malcolm Haines, age thirty, of no fixed address
Left in a tractor-trailer, number two, headin' west
He had fifty thousand cans of beer, for a depot in TO
Part of a greater shipment of Moosehead for Mexico

Emmet Bresnahan, "The Moose Is Loose"

CONTENTS

Dedicated to loyal Moosehead lovers from around the world.

ACKNOWLEDGEMENTS

The *Beer Bandit Caper* could not have come together without the cooperation, assistance, good humour, and sincerity of many people. Thanks first to Nimbus Publishing's Dan Soucoup and Sandra McIntyre for the invitation to research and write the book, and to Sandra for her editorial insights and guidance. Thanks also to Terrilee Bulger, Heather Bryan, Penelope Jackson, and James MacNevin at Nimbus. And to the following individuals: Joel Levesque and Bruce Robinson at Moosehead Breweries, Saint John, NB; Jeff Lake of Cirrus Communications, Toronto; Gerardo Arturo Rodriguez Campollo, Soriana corporation, Monterrey, Nuevo Leon, Mexico; Maria Arcelus of Fredericton, NB; RCMP Corporal Kevin Jackson, Oromocto, NB; RCMP Sergeant Paul Brown, Blackville, NB; Bob Myers and Maurice Gaudet, Westmoreland Institution, Dorchester, NB; Crown prosecutor and writer Cameron Gunn, Fredericton; defence lawyer Ron Morris, Fredericton; Owen Lawson, East Newbridge, NB; Ralph Boyd, Atlantic Provinces Trucking Association, Moncton, NB; songwriter Emmet Bresnahan, St. Stephen, NB; Julie Caswell, ATV, Halifax; Don MacPherson, Fredericton *Daily Gleaner*; syndicated cartoonist Michael de Adder, Halifax; Theresa Reid, Rusagonis, NB; photographer Stephen MacGillivray, Fredericton; Brad and Judy Mills, Fredericton; and Burton Green, Fredericton.

Special thanks to George Piers at the Fredericton Community Kitchen for his candour and insights.

And finally to Wade Haines for his open-minded approach to the project. I wish him all the best.

PART I

THE MOOSE GETS LOOSE

THE NEWS RELIEF

August 18, 2004, seemed destined to be just another dry news day. Even news, it seems, takes a vacation. It took the unpremeditated actions of a previously obscure New Brunswicker to stir news editors from Fredericton to Vancouver to Atlanta from their summer hiatus, their mid-August siesta. The ruckus began that day after two successive news releases were issued from two different sources.

The first volley was lobbed in the morning from the public affairs office of Moosehead Breweries in Saint John, New Brunswick. The company's PR whiz, Joel Levesque, sprang the story in concert with Jeff Lake, the company's Toronto-based public relations consultant. They made a calculated decision to go public over the disappearance of a truckload of Moosehead Lager. They determined that such a release carried no foreseeable downside. They were never more right in their careers.

Fifty thousand cans of Spanish-labelled, Mexico-bound Moosehead Lager had gone missing, starting a cycle in which lots more beer (of the English-labelled variety) would be sold in a truly novel way: using a fortuitous crime as a marketing hook. In fairness to Moosehead, it was out of their hands. There had been no promotional premeditation, no brainstorming session where the ad and PR guys conjured up a campaign theme predicated on theft. As they used to jest on TV's *Laugh In*, it was "the Fickle Finger of Fate." As hungry yet responsible PR guys, they had no choice. While the Molson, Labatt, and Sleeman's sales teams spent time wishing they could have suffered the ordeal of a news-generating beer heist, Moosehead was heading free-fall into the greatest media landslide in the company's history. The story erupted in response to this simple text:

> *For Immediate Release*
> *Saint John, NB—August 18, 2004—If you're offered a*
> *Moosehead Lager in the next few days and it has English and*
> *Spanish labelling, there's a very good chance it's been stolen.*
>   *A truck loaded with 8,400 six-packs of cans of Moosehead*
> *Lager left Fredericton Sunday evening for Toronto en route to*
> *Mexico, where the beer was to be distributed. The abandoned*
> *tractor-trailer was found empty at noon yesterday behind a*
> *McDonalds restaurant in Grand Falls, New Brunswick....*
> *New Brunswick RCMP have issued a Canada-wide search for*
> *the driver, after attempts to reach him by Moosehead and the*
> *driver's trucking company went unanswered Monday when the*
> *truck failed to arrive in Toronto. The retail value of the missing*
> *beer is just over $70,000.*

An hour away in Oromocto, members of the Royal Canadian Mounted Police discussed with the best straight face they could muster what they should do about a truckload of missing beer, the disappearance of the truck's driver, and Moosehead's announcement. Within hours, a second release was issued, this one by officials stationed at the Oromocto RCMP detachment:

RCMP investigate missing beer delivery
Oromocto District 2 RCMP is investigating the report of a
truckload of missing beer. A tractor-trailer load of Moosehead
beer being trucked to Toronto from Saint John was discovered
at the mall in Grand Falls, N.B. on August 17, 2004 at 6:40
P.M. The truck was carrying more than 4,000 cases of beer. 20
cases were found inside the trailer. The rest are missing. The
driver, 30-year-old Wade Haines, has not been located.

The more than 50,000 cans have English labeling on one
side and Spanish on the other and were destined for the
Mexico market.

Anyone with information is asked to contact the District 2
Oromocto RCMP at 506-357-4300 or NB Crime Stoppers at
1-800-222-8477 (TIPS).

On the heels of those communiqués, Wade Haines was thrust into his fifteen minutes of fame. Lazy summer newswires turned to crazy. The story began to buzz. The Beer Bandit caper enlivened newsrooms with a level of oomph that is normally reserved for celebrity scandal. It was the kind of event that makes everything in its wake seem surreal, off the wall, and quirky. In Toronto, one can imagine CBC news anchor Peter Mansbridge on the day the story broke, rubbing his chin in amusement, wondering where to place the item in the news lineup. Even Rex Murphy would have difficulty finding the right words for one of his biting, esoteric editorials.

Further afield, during live international hurricane coverage being fed from Florida, CNN's decision desk in Atlanta couldn't resist the temptation to stripe the bottom of the rain-speckled, blustery screen with continuous references to the Beer Bandit heist. Canadians everywhere would high-five, congratulating one another for finally having a story of their own on the mother of cable news networks.

Within twenty-four hours of the initial press releases, the story that would come to be known as the Beer Bandit caper was the most talked-about happening in Atlantic Canada, if not the entire country. Beer-guzzling Canadian bar-dwellers welcomed this diversion from the endless drone of the pending NHL lockout. Office workers sprang forth from the late-summer boredom of their water coolers to celebrate their liberation from mundane small talk about the weather, if only for a few days. The revised forecast called for several fronts of silly stories from the east and a succession of storm clouds over Wade Haines.

Mientras tanto, en Mexico
MEANWHILE IN MEXICO

Hard at work, the thirsty blue-collar workers of Ciudad Juárez, Mexico, let their minds drift. They're having daydreams about beer things in the middle of the afternoon. It's a typical Mexican afternoon: a flaming, Lucifer, high-noon beast of a day.

Meanwhile, another horned beast—the outdoorsy, wilderness-loving, car-accident-prone icon whose smug mug is profiled on every can of Moosehead—is playing a starring role in the workers' daydreams. The head of a moose? In Mexico? It's as random and out-of-context in Latin America as a Newfoundland sealer at a Greenpeace convention. It's like Canadians waking up one day to chihuahua-branded donut shops.

But yes, Mexico, it is so. The combination of market timing, price, and taste have created a minor craze for Saint John's frothy pride and joy. Already a favoured beer of Maritimers wherever they roam, it is now, strangely, tops with such unexpected markets as Mexicans and Hawaiian surfers. *Si, Señor*! Righteous, dude!

The hardworking, daydreaming men of Juárez toil with the confidence that their wives are at the local Soriana "hypermarket," where a small flood of those luxuriously pure, golden, northern suds awaits. The men envision arriving home from their labour, followed by the joyful experience of Moosehead beer cascading down the backs of their sorely parched throats.

At a Juárez Soriana outlet, at the end of the busy centre aisle, a young man pleads for patience.

"But Señora, I am just a stock boy."

As they scold and heap needless disdain upon the helpless young man, two particularly cantankerous women stand out from an angry throng of customers, tugging ferociously on the last twenty-four-can case of Moosehead Lager.

"This is a crime," says one. "I demand to speak to the manager. The flyer said *cerveza* Moosehead for twenty pesos."

While she complains to the innocent young stock clerk, her determined, feisty opponent wins the tug-of-war, nearly falls on the slippery floor tiles, then rushes down the aisle, turning out of sight toward the Soriana meat section.

"There!" she bellows. "Another crime at the hands of that woman. I am robbed right here in Soriana, in broad daylight. With witnesses!"

As the empty-handed patron continues berating the bewildered young clerk, the remainder of the throng disperses in frustration, flailing their arms and their tongues. The store's duty manager arrives on the scene to console the remaining irate customer. He is determined to sort out whatever is the matter. The customer has a familiar face. The manager knows her by name and by reputation for being difficult.

"There now, Señora Perez. What seems to be the problem?"

The patron gives him a piece of her mind over the falsely advertised special, and then proceeds to blame the store for the actions of her opponent in the Moosehead tug-of-war. Mrs. Perez's opponent is now seen scurrying by the end of the aisle en route from meats to the snacks section.

"But Señora Perez, how can you pick on this young man. Alvarez is just a stock boy. He does not deal with such matters. He does not know where the Moosehead beer is, because nobody knows where the Moosehead beer is. It has been stolen. Stolen in Canada by a beer bandit. It is on CNN."

The patron looks in disbelief at the manager.

"Stolen in Canada? But it is such a safe country. Canada has bandits?"

"Apparently so. Beer bandits. The Moosehead beer has disappeared. So we await another shipment in a matter of days. I am very sorry."

Mrs. Perez looks at Alvarez the stock boy, feeling embarrassed.

"I am sorry young man. Who would believe that there are such things as beer bandits in Canada. I will return on Friday. Hopefully by then…"

"Hopefully by then, Señora Perez we will have enough Moosehead for everyone. Thank you for coming. You have a nice day."

This episode is fictional but not unlikely. In working-class Mexico, the woman of the house typically does the grocery shopping: there are remnants here of that fabled 1950s America where full-time housewives were the norm and men brought home the bacon.

It is common for beer, the liquid staple, to be mixed into the shopping cart with the family staples, unlike in Atlantic Canada where beer, wine and spirits are more strictly controlled. And beer is commonly on the "to-get" list of the Mexican shopper. Carts at the Juárez Soriana outlet are frequently topped with a case or two or three of the newly beloved Moosehead Lager. The women's objective: to quench their husbands' thirsts, to keep their hard working men happy. And Moosehead's been one of the most popular thirst-quenching choices since the company's international sales guys began penetrating the vast market south of the US border in December of 2002.

The Soriana stores look like any large-scale grocery chain store you'd see in Texas or California, complete with modern exteriors, superbly effective signage and world-class merchandising. The company goes head-to-head in the Mexican market with Wal-Mart, after all. But in spite of the incredible size and selection available at Soriana, including dozens of competing beer brands, Moosehead has somehow developed a true following.

Mexican brews are great for scorching hot days. They're patio and beach beers. Guinness they are not, because when the temperature soars, no one wants to consume an intense, heavy brew that looks like espresso. That's where Mexican beer—*cerveza* in Spanish—comes into play. Moosehead, being a lager, is akin to the Mexican stuff because it's made with a type of yeast that rests at the bottom of the liquid after fermentation. Lager ferments at lower temperatures than the top-fermenting yeasts used to make ales. Moosehead Lager, therefore, like its cousin Corona, tends to be smoother, cleaner, and more subtle than ales, giving it natural appeal with Mexican consumers.

Given the high Mexican demand for Moosehead, one can imagine how, within a short time of the Beer Bandit heist, an abrupt hiccup must have occurred in the regular flow of the beer throughout the Soriana chain, which is the sole distributor of Moosehead in all of Mexico. A vacuum in the brand's traditional display space must have appeared. One can imagine, therefore, that in the Juárez outlet and dozens of other stores throughout the chain, only scant, vestigial cases of Moosehead would have remained on display. Or, as in the case of our fictional female customers, perhaps just the one case worth fighting over.

Things Go Crazier with Coke

If you got bad news and you wanna kick them blues; cocaine.
When your day is done and you wanna run; cocaine.
She don't lie, she don't lie, she don't lie; cocaine.
   Eric Clapton, "Cocaine"

There's a bold sign with black letters against a yellow background outside the offices of Brenway Transport in Fredericton, which reads: "Quality Drivers Wanted." It does not say "Straight and Sober Drivers Wanted," but if you read between the lines, that's what it implies. Wade Haines need not re-apply.

On the weekend of the Beer Bandit heist, things in Haines's life really became unravelled. He morphed into a living, breathing country song, a Nashville cliché of the highest order: a truck stolen, a girl lost, a glut of drugs and alcohol, no money except for an illicitly cashed cheque, and a looming jail sentence for fraud charges. Thankfully, Haines did not own a dog.

In what he calls his "diminished capacity," a condition he developed between August 11 and 15, everything loomed large. He'd hardly slept a wink during those five days, he'd been riding high on cocaine, drinking rye whisky, and he was distraught over most things in his personal life.

So who is Wade Malcolm Haines?

He is actually a pretty articulate guy, as most people who know him would attest, a guy with a sense of humour, a guy who's up on things. He knows, for example, what the latest Michael Crichton novel is titled; he's interested, because of my book project, in such abstract things as copyright; and he's got a basic grip on the comings and goings of the legal system. Just because things haven't necessarily gone his way in court doesn't mean he's judicially vacant. In spite of his being aware and articulate, however, he has been known to suffer from over-confidence. And in the third week of August 2004, he coupled this over-confidence with a double dose of "diminished capacity." Diminished capacity is not a recognized medical condition. It is an attitude, a feeling, a rarefied state that results from self-abuse, from self-torture. Diminished capacity is at its worst when you are also in a mountain of shit with your boss, your girlfriend, and the law.

This highly toxic recipe for generating bad judgment sent Haines headlong into a brier patch of demoralizing circumstances on that not-so-august August weekend. Not only was there that pending fraud charge, but he'd also gone and cashed a paycheque that was supposed to have been lost and cancelled, an act certain to result in the loss of his job even if the news of his fraud trial didn't. As if all that wasn't sufficiently demoralizing, his on-again, off-again, long-time girlfriend, Cari Watson, had just informed him that she was pregnant. Exacerbating that particular problem was the news that the seed had apparently not come from the loins of Wade Haines. This buzzing, humming hive of troubles set in motion a series of events that resulted, one way or another, in the disappearance of the fifty thousand cans of Spanish-labelled Moosehead Lager and a Brenway tractor-trailer, which were, as the RCMP so aptly put it, "under the care and control" of Mr. Haines.

With all of its unlikely tangents and curious characters, it is impossible to discuss the Beer Bandit caper with a straight face. It's a tale so infectious that it's hard to resist being drawn into the nuttiness of it all. Consider, for example, the small but humorous fact that Haines does not even drink beer. (There is the distinct possibility, however, that some of his acquaintances do.)

Although he's the guy who at thirty-one made the international newswires for his involvement in the Beer Bandit heist, like everyone, he was once just a kid. He used to deliver the Fredericton *Daily Gleaner*, which in later years would picture him in handcuffs, above the fold on page one. He played football, hockey, and soccer. He worked at Pizza Hut at fifteen. He attended Fredericton and Oromocto high schools. He cooked and washed dishes at a city-area hotel, worked as a laborer in concrete and construction, and finally ended up in Edmonton, Alberta, where he fell in love with driving truck. It was out west, in Edmonton, where Haines took a professional truck-driving course and where he gained "mountain experience," as he calls it. Learning to drive big rigs in the Rockies means you learn how to shift like nobody's business, or perish in a heap at the base of some hard-to-negotiate hairpin turn.

He has seen his natural father, who lives in Georgetown, Ontario, only twice in his life. Because his mother, Theresa, was frequently busy trying to figure out the rest of her life—according to Haines, she had to drop out of university while pregnant, and, among other things, had to drive cab after he was born—Haines was sent to live with his maternal grandparents, Alan and Doris Maunder. Living with them off and on in Lower St. Mary's, a section of Fredericton, was not such a bad thing, he says, although there was periodic evidence of the forty-odd-year generation gap. They died in 1995, just fifty-one days apart, Alan at sixty-seven from complications due to diabetes, Doris at sixty-nine from what was believed to be cancer. Haines says without hesitation that he loved them.

Haines has two children, boy and girl twins, who were born in 1997. They live with their mother, with whom Haines has little if any contact.

He has been "known to police" for years, his forte being fraud and theft. But it's not much of a forte: he's had something on the order of a dozen convictions, all involving taking what's not rightfully his, in one form or another. As Haines puts it: "I'm a good cement finisher and I'm a good truck driver, but I'm a lousy criminal."

Most serious among his previous offences was a 1993 conviction for fraud, primarily writing bad cheques, for which he served eight months in a New Brunswick provincial institution. In January 2004, he was sentenced to five months for stealing jewellery. Drugs have been at the heart of it all.

Having become familiarized with Haines, one naturally becomes curious about the events surrounding the Beer Bandit heist and the emergence of his self-diagnosed "diminished capacity." At the core of the story is Haines's missing sleep. Scientists say we lose our faculties without it; applying the word "deprivation" makes it sound more like a condition or a disease.

On the morning of Wednesday, August 11, 2004, Haines was assigned to drive from Doaktown, on the Miramichi River, northward to Shippegan, a lively little fishing community on New Brunswick's Acadian Peninsula. By lunchtime, his Brenway trailer was loaded full of peat moss destined for Montreal. He arrived in the Quebec metropolis at two or three in the morning on Thursday, August 12, and nabbed a slight trickle of Zs in his truck's sleeper compartment. First thing that morning, the truck was unloaded and Haines awaited his dispatch instructions from the Fredericton Brenway office. At four o'clock that afternoon, he arrived at the Schenley spirits processing plant in Montreal, where he oversaw the loading of twenty-four pallets of Crown Royal whisky, a shipment whose value he estimates as $400,000 to $500,000. It was normal for Haines to be running the Trans-Canada two to three times a week, hauling Schenley or Seagrams products, including such commodities as Crown Royal, Dr. McGillicuddy's, Stella Artois, and ironically, Sol beer from Mexico. In other words, it was normal for Haines to haul commodities of a much higher value than Moosehead beer.

With the cache of hard liquor onboard, Haines drove from Montreal to Fredericton for a 7:00 A.M. delivery at the New Brunswick Liquor Commission's warehouse in the city's industrial park. He was, as he tells it, "the first one in there." He says he returned to the Brenway Transport yard on Fredericton's Hanwell Road and spent the morning shunting three more parked and fully loaded trailers to the liquor corporation warehouse.

"At lunchtime, I just wanted to go home and go to bed," says Haines.

But the folks at Brenway asked him to take on a shipment destined for Toronto on Monday. This being his first Toronto trip for Brenway, Haines says he didn't want to turn the opportunity down, even though he was flat-out exhausted. Although the shipment wasn't due in Toronto until Monday, a full three days later, the goods had to be loaded that afternoon at the Moosehead production plant in Saint John, an hour and fifteen minutes away. Next thing he knew, the sleep deprivation now starting to seriously sink in, Haines was negotiating an empty trailer into the loading dock of Moosehead Breweries.

Around four o'clock on Friday the 13th, the beer load-out was finished. The trailer was full to the brim with Spanish-labelled Moosehead Lager—the soon-to-be-infamous fifty thousand cans. Although he was now suffering from a near-desperate sleep deficiency, Haines was still driving, albeit in the company of a buddy, a fellow who is also rumoured to have experienced a day or two in jail in his time. They dropped the trailer off in Brenway's Fredericton yard. In spite of his weakened condition, Haines somehow reasoned, or was persuaded, that it would be a good thing to conduct a tour of Fredericton's circuit of drug houses for a buffet of cocaine and grass. He swears he had nothing to drink during that first night of recklessness. Moreover, he claims to have been pretty much off cocaine since November of 2003, with the exception of two weekend binges.

He spent Friday night crashing at someone's house in Taymouth, just a few kilometres from the New Brunswick capital. Remember: in spite of his increasingly diminished capacity, he was still driving the Brenway truck.

The next morning—Saturday—Haines arose and eventually went to the friend's yard to start the truck, to no avail.

This was a critical turning point in the weekend. With the truck sitting there deader than a doornail, Haines had no choice but to call Brenway, resulting in the arrival of a very pissed-off maintenance guy who'd had to interrupt his weekend to drive the twenty minutes out to Taymouth. At seven-thirty that evening, the unhappy mechanic scolded Haines for having parked the truck on an incline, thereby draining one of the two fuel tanks into the other and leaving the carburetor and the fuel system dry as a bone. Truckers, when sober, apparently know that this is not good practice. Haines and the mechanic had words, giving Haines one more thing to worry about.

In addition to this argument, there was the matter of the cocaine he'd ingested, the grass he'd smoked, and the sleep he'd deprived himself of. All this while still other matters were unfolding in the background.

A paycheque for around $500 that had been issued to Haines that week had gone missing. He'd convinced the company's bean counters to issue a second cheque while a stop-payment was placed on the initial one. Lo and behold, the first cheque re-emerged, crumpled inside the pocket of Haines's freshly laundered pants. In the depths of his diminished capacity, Haines set about convincing a friend's mother to cash the cancelled cheque.

Haines knows that the friend's mother remains "pissed. I owe her the five hundred dollars," he freely admits. Asked how he could have taken the woman's money, Haines again points to his diminished capacity and confesses with simplicity: "I needed it."

So the fraudulent cashing of the cancelled cheque was on his mind. Also on his mind was a court appearance, scheduled for Monday morning, on charges connected to the theft of a video camera from a Fredericton pawnshop called Digital World. Haines says he had arranged for his friend John Faust to appear on his behalf because he was supposed to be arriving in Toronto with the truckload of Mexico-destined beer. The fraudulent cashing of the cancelled cheque aside, Haines knew that once Brenway Transport's management caught wind of the video camera theft, he'd be fired immediately—"on the spot" as they say.

And of course there was Cari Watson's news that she was pregnant with someone else's child.

This melting pot of anxiety called for a second night of touring Fredericton's drug houses. Haines and someone else who was in his company met up with a chap named Andy Copp, an admitted cocaine addict with a prosthetic leg, who spent nearly all of a quarter-million-dollar insurance settlement on drugs. Haines says Copp wanted a drive to a dealer's house in the Brenway semi. Back and forth they went between 11:00 P.M. and 2:00 A.M., buying just a little coke at a time. Unlike the previous night, on the Saturday Haines was drinking rye in addition to getting stoned. His capacity was, by now, about as diminished as it could get.

A thumb goes up, a car goes by
Oh, won't somebody stop and help a guy,
Hitchin' a ride, hitchin' a ride,
Been away too long, from my baby's side.
   Vanity Fair, "Hitchin A Ride"

The next morning—Sunday—Haines says he drove, in his stupor and state of anxiety, from north Fredericton to the south side, parked, left the keys in the truck, and began to hitchhike. He says he was given a ride by a male francophone from Quebec with a black, 2002 Ford F-150.

The man in the Ford went as far as Cabano, Quebec. Haines says he recalls then walking and hitchhiking, perhaps as long as four hours. He was picked up by two French women in their forties driving a red Sunbird. The three drove together for only fifteen minutes before Haines was dropped at a convenience store. But it was enough to get Haines close to Rivière-du-Loup. He was so tired, he didn't really care that he had to camp in the woods on Sunday night.

On Monday, Haines hitched yet another ride into Rivière-du-Loup, where he stayed at a motel whose name he can't recall. He does remember that the Quebec town has what he calls "two main drags," one near a Wal-Mart store, the other closer to the river. The motel, he believes, was on the main drag closest to the river. He recalls minor things about his time there, like having a pizza.

On Tuesday morning, Haines walked to the bus station, situated at a Le Normandin outlet, bought a ticket and took the bus to Montreal. From there, his bussing trek continued when he bought a ticket to Peterborough, Ontario, by way of Ottawa. His only sustenance during this time was a steady diet of snacks from bus-terminal vending machines.

Aunt Susan and Uncle Randy live in Lindsay, Ontario, with Haines's twenty-four-year-old cousin, Jana. Susan is the natural sister-in-law of Haines's father, meaning she is not a blood relative, but one that Haines feels connected to nevertheless. He feels similarly connected to his cousin Jana, and he has a lot in common with "Uncle" Randy because they both understand and love trucks.

As evidence that he intended to return to Fredericton, Haines explains that Uncle Randy had arranged for a drive with a guy delivering cattle as far as Quebec City. From there, having access to a CB radio, Haines says he would have had no difficulty getting drives all the way home.

"I was not running away from anything in particular," says Haines, adding that it was the cloud of everything on the weekend of August 13–15 that messed him up. "I had every intention of coming back." He spent his time in Lindsay with Jana, going to bars in the evening and "just hanging out," he says.

Meanwhile, Haines's extended family was tuning in to the national news and discovering that Haines was a "missing person." The chain of inter-family communications that followed makes one wonder about the family members' internal loyalties. A cousin in Alberta caught the news and telephoned Haines's natural grandfather's wife in Ontario. She in turn called Aunt Susan in Lindsay and learned that Haines was present there. The RCMP, in turn, called Susan on August 23 and instructed her not to advise Haines of their contact. They'd been alerted to his whereabouts by Haines's use of a Brenway Tranport calling card. Haines says he'd begun to suspect that Susan knew about the manhunt, because even he had learned through a copy of the Toronto *Sun* that he was a missing person. Susan finally admitted to Haines that the RCMP were en route from New Brunswick. He simply awaited their arrival.

THE MOUNTIES

RCMP Corporal Kevin Jackson, a native of Shelburne, Nova Scotia, has been in policing since 1986 when he joined the Canadian military for a three-year stint. He became a counsellor for young offenders for a year, but during his military sojourn, he applied to the RCMP. He's been in the force since 1990, posted to such detachments as Placentia, Newfoundland; Northern Labrador, where he policed Hopedale and the infamous Davis Inlet; Holyrood near St. John's; Avalon East; Campobello Island; and Minto-Chipman in New Brunswick. He became the team leader of the Oromocto detachment in July of 2004, just six weeks prior to the Beer Bandit heist.

In Jackson's opinion, the Beer Bandit case was not all that extraordinary. "It never stood outside the box really, for me, personally," he says. "The issue, of course, was that the Mexican Moosehead beer thing really took off as a media hook. I think we realized that within the first couple of weeks of the investigation, but we were still quite surprised how quick that took off and how far it went as well, around the world.

"I've worked on different cases that are odd, strange and could be considered a little stranger than this," he adds. "There are so many cases that I've been involved in that it's a blur really."

Jackson says it's not necessarily all that unusual for a tractor-trailer full of stuff to go missing in Canada, even if it's not a regular occurrence in the province of New Brunswick.

According to Jackson, it was on August 23 that he and Pierre Gervais, the RCMP's lead investigator for the Beer Bandit case, first learned that Wade Haines was in Lindsay. They left New

Brunswick on the 23rd, arrived in Lindsay on the 24th, and set up an interview with Wade Haines later that day.

"We were surprised with the public knowledge or public awareness of the case two provinces away from the eastern part of Canada," says Jackson. "It was evident to us that we weren't there long and the general public realized that, you know, here are the Mounties; the Mounties are in our town, and they're investigating this Mexican Moosehead beer heist."

Although they drove an unmarked car, the two Mounties couldn't escape the public's curiosity. "We had stopped at a gas station to pick up a few things before we went back to the motel," recalls Jackson. "It was actually Pierre Gervais who was confronted by somebody in the community and talked to him about the case and realized why we were there."

Apart from the one direct encounter, Jackson and Gervais had a general sense of being noticed. "There were a lot of people waving to us in the community," says Jackson.

The officers telephoned the house where Haines was visiting and his aunt took the call.

Rather than surprising Haines at the house, the Mounties invited him to the local police station for an interview. Haines accepted their invitation.

When Jackson and Gervais had Haines in a room at the local police station, there were two segments to their discussion: the interview and a subsequent interrogation, which lasted for three to four hours. It was a lengthy process, according to Cpl. Jackson, but the interrogation was pretty standard.

Haines says that one of the questions he remembers best from the interrogation was, "What were your intentions?" He says that as he tried to review the events of August 13, 14, and 15, he simply didn't have any sense of recall, presumably because of his diminished capacity.

As for Haines's story, that he abandonned the truck and had nothing to do with the subsequent theft, the Mounties weren't buying it.

"In relation to his statement, the story was pretty far-fetched," argues Jackson. "After I conducted the interview portion of the statement I realized it was not going to wash. Police work in my opinion is very simple. All we're here to do is seek the truth. That's all we're here to do. We're not here to embellish anything or anything of that nature. And it's very easy to see when the truth doesn't add up. When you get a series of facts before you and you're interviewing somebody and the ends aren't meeting...well...that's what happened in this case. He parked his trailer in this state [i.e., in his diminished capacity]. He left his tractor in another part of the city in this state. Coincidentally, somebody steals the tractor, [and] coincidentally, marries it up with the trailer that he parked a few days prior. It just didn't wash."

Jackson thinks Haines was overly confident about "his ability to pull the wool over law enforcement's eyes." In Jackson's opinion, it's that excessive confidence that caused Haines's downfall, leading him to make statements that resulted in his conviction.

Following the interrogation, Haines was arrested in Lindsay and remanded into custody. Jackson, Gervais, and Haines drove back to Fredericton on August 25 and 26. In spite of his professional experience, Haines did none of the driving.

By all accounts, Haines was cooperative during the trip, and no cuffs or shackles were needed. Jackson interprets this as a sign that Haines "was still maintaining his confidence level even at that point."

The three drove straight through to New Brunswick, stopping only for bathroom breaks and sustenance. With every passing kilometre, Jackson and Gervais were inching Haines nearer to becoming the most talked-about criminal figure in the Maritimes. Along the way, there was small talk—mostly about the trucking industry, according to Jackson. "He was telling us basically how it operated, the different trucking companies, different truck stops along the way, where they regularly stopped and things of that nature."

The only stop of note that Jackson could recall was at an A&W restaurant where they bought their supper.

Jackson was already confident about the interview, the inter-rogation and arrest he'd supervised in Lindsay, and the inevitable trial. His confidence was rooted in Haines's verbosity during the interrogation. "The statement provided by Wade Haines was defi-nitely an important aspect of the investigation," he claims. "Now with that statement, we had the opportunity to either prove or dis-prove what he had stated through our investigation and that meant taking every little piece of information that we got and looking at it and determining if in fact it was true or not, or following up any little lead we had, so after we obtained the statement from him it was a matter of good old fashioned police work. I know it's used all the time, but it was not leaving any stone unturned and chasing everything down."

The Mounties interviewed more than thirty people to build their case. There were initially a half dozen members of the force involved in the investigation to varying degrees. Once matters con-gealed, the investigation was more exclusively in the hands of then Constable, now Corporal, Pierre Gervais. As is normal, Gervais had periodic peripheral support from members in Oromocto and in other detachments.

Personally, Jackson believes that there were others involved in the Beer Bandit caper, and that Haines is protecting their identi-ties. "I think I'm disappointed in Wade Haines for not telling the truth," he says, "for not putting everything out on the table. I know that there's this unwritten rule that you can't rat out your friends type of thing, but I think that's more of a movie scenario than the actual fact. If he felt he couldn't give us the complete truth and put it on the table for fear of injury or anything of that nature, I don't see that."

"I wasn't there to know who was involved," Haines still insisted after several months of incarceration.

He says it's not so much that he held and kept "the code"; it's that all he's got is hearsay about who took the shipment while he was in the depths of his sleep-deprived, cocaine-fuelled, rye-whisky spree. He does readily acknowledge that he probably had too much to say about the beer shipment to too many people.

When news of the missing beer first broke, police thought they might have had a murder case on their hands. "I think initially why we had the resources on it that we did," explains Jackson, "is that we didn't know if Wade Haines was dead or alive. We didn't know if it was a hijacking initially because we hadn't heard from him. That was our first concern. Was this guy murdered? Where is he? We have a missing person. That's a lot more important than a truckload of beer. And that becomes our foremost focus in an investigation."

Haines's criminal past was not the issue, Jackson maintains. "Regardless of somebody's past, we have to look out for their welfare if they're missing."

Jackson says that with both Haines and the truckload of beer missing, there were a lot of different possibilities for police to consider. "A case like that is treated like a murder until we prove otherwise. Once we discover where the individual is, well okay fine, then we can cut it back a notch and we progress on with the property-related offence."

The rest of the case, says Jackson, is closed. "We've basically exhausted all of our leads and once we've exhausted all of our leads and no further evidence is forthcoming, we have to make a decision on all our investigations whether or not to conclude them. And just because a file is concluded, doesn't mean that it cannot be reopened in the future. And in this case, the best way to reopen the case is to have Wade Haines walk through the door and tell us the complete truth and about everybody that was involved."

Jackson is not holding his breath.

Regarding the durability of the case as a media event, Jackson says, "it has a life of its own, but I think it's because it has so much media play that the general public have the intimate details of it and find it interesting and find it a subject of interest."

As an example, Jackson points to the public's continuing fascination with the Sapnish-labelled Moosehead itself. "It wasn't a couple of weeks ago [in May 2005], somebody had discovered an empty can of Mexican Moosehead beer along the side of a highway, so they brought it into us from Wasiis. So they came in with this empty can of Mexican Moosehead beer. You know, if it was any other type of beer, we'd never see it.

"I think a considerable amount of it [the beer] is destroyed by now," he continues. "They dumped a lot of it in the Millville area. There's too much heat around it. A little too much police scrutiny in relation to it. We've had information from various sources in regards to where some of the beer ended up and how it's being distributed and things of that nature. So there still could be a portion of it out there."

As for the question of who provided the evidence that helped put Haines behind bars, Jackson says that, in his experience, people who get convicted almost never have an accurate understanding of who did the informing. "I have yet to see anybody that we've ever charged with an offence or interviewed or suspected of committing an offence, see them even hit close to the mark in relation to identifying who the informant is. They think they do all the time but I haven't seen it."

Strangely, Haines thinks that in one respect, the police investigation wasn't very complete. Forget the irony that he probably didn't tell everything he knew. As he puts it, "they did not recover any of the beer. The police never found any beer. Somebody had it really well hid."

The beer that did emerge as evidence, Haines points out, was brought forward by citizens—such as four pallets of cans that went flying into farmer Owen Lawson's East Newbridge bull pasture, and a small cache of lager found along the Miramichi that came to light when the Blackville RCMP were shown a single can of the beer found at a nearby marijuana grow op.

THE UNDER-ARRESTED

Wade Haines was not necessarily a scapegoat. As Cpl. Jackson points out, it was Haines who had control of the truck full of lager on Friday, August 13, 2004. He wasn't exactly just some innocent passerby, like a naïve backpacker who unwittingly carts drugs into Thailand. But still, everyone, including the RCMP, readily admits that Haines couldn't possibly have acted without the help of others. So why on earth weren't the others charged? Many people claim that the cops must know full well who the others are. Given today's criminology techniques, they probably know what the others eat for breakfast, lunch, and dinner. There is one theory: the others are bigger fish, fish that the cops will fry when the time is right.

In the overall scheme of things, the Beer Bandit heist was small potatoes, peanuts, amateur night, kindergarten, juice-and-cracker time, the five-and-dime. It was small-town stuff. And, according to the theory, it's drugs, not beer, that the cops want; the others involved in the theft and redistribution of the beer are probably also involved in the drug trade. If these others had been charged and convicted for beer theft, they'd have gotten nothing compared to the lengthy jail terms they'll get for drug charges.

So, as the other Moosehead-guzzling bad guys laugh about having gotten away with robbery, the Mounties just might be sitting patiently, hands clasped and fingers woven together across the front of their bullet-resistant vests, thumbs moving in Tiddlywinks rotation, biding their collective time. Like the best of fishers, they await the big catch. It could all come down to drugs, surer convictions, and longer sentences—sentences measured in years, not weeks. If this theory is true, it will make the Mounties' risks seem all the more worthwhile.

BANDITS, BANDIDOS, BURGLARS, OUTLAWS, DESPERADOES, AND HIGHWAYMEN

Not to excuse Wade Haines in the least, but there are worse things one can do than steal—things like cannibalism, grave-robbing, stalking, treason, and kidnapping. The ranking and classifying of criminal acts is a complicated affair. According to natural law theory, for instance, criminality and illegality are separate and distinct categories: the former is derived from human nature, and includes those acts that violate individual liberty; the latter is derived from the interests of those in power. The two are sometimes expressed with the Latin terms *malum in se*, which describes acts that are inherently criminal, and *malum prohibitum*, which describes acts that are criminal only because the law has decreed them to be so, like homosexuality, which remains an offence in some jurisdictions. This presents a paradox, because some acts can be illegal but not criminal, while some criminal acts can be perfectly legal. But enough of the academic viewpoint.

Society loves to brand and categorize its varied types of misfits, and our culture has a long history of fascination with criminals. To take a prominent example, there are highwaymen, a term that emerged in Britain during the seventeenth and eighteenth centuries to describe criminals who robbed people travelling by stagecoach and other modes of transport along public "highways"—which were actually rutted dirt roads. Your typical highwayman rode a horse, carried a pistol, wore high leather boots, and commanded his victims to "stand and deliver." Sometimes, he uttered the phrase: "Your money or your life." Sometimes, he rode away with a victim damsel. Sometimes, the victim damsel was all the happier for a little adventure, but this was usually not the case.

The highwaymen went the way of the road, so to speak, during the early half of the nineteenth century when better roads, better law enforcement, and banking reforms cut into their potential for profit, and diminished their chances of getting away. But the highwaymen have at least one thing in common with latter-day bandits: the Hollywood romanticization of their work and their personalities. As a result, they are often imagined to be free-spirited rogues who love their women, their wine, and other people's moolah. Many bandits and highwaymen have been glorified; they are feared and loathed by those in power, yet worshipped by the underclass.

Even though he didn't stick anybody up as such, Wade Haines could be loosely branded as a modern-day highwayman, a breed of criminal that is particularly frightening to the trucking industry but enjoys a sizeable fan base in the media and on the street. Because of this deep cultural resonance, the Beer Bandit heist came to seem like an odd form of reality entertainment. As a culture, we relish the refined techniques and dark romance of the burglar; there's something wonderfully voyeuristic about it. And there are criminals in our culture that we definitely cheer for. We're with Danny Ocean all the way to the bank. It made for great theatre when Warren Beatty and Faye Dunaway gyrated as they got machine-gunned to death in *Bonnie and Clyde*, but we were sad to see them go. They'd become endeared to us. We cheered for each successful heist in spite of the bodies of cops and random bystanders left shot and strewn in their wake. In light of this, is it any wonder that the Beer Bandit caper captured the popular imagination in the way that it did?

Along with the highwayman, another prominent character in the cultural history of crime is the outlaw. In the common law tradition, an outlaw was a person who defied the laws of the realm by such acts as ignoring a summons to court or fleeing instead of appearing to plead when charged with a crime. In the earlier law of Anglo-Saxon England, outlawry was also declared when a person committed a homicide and could not pay the blood money due to the victim's kin. Outlawry also existed in other legal codes of earlier times, such as the ancient Norse and Icelandic codes.

To be declared an outlaw was to suffer a form of "civil death," to be exiled from civilized society. No one would be permitted to step in to provide an outlaw with food, shelter, or any other support. To do so was to be *couthutlaugh*, or aiding and abetting, and to be in danger of the same bans. A person who encountered an outlaw was allowed, indeed encouraged, to kill him. Because the outlaw had defiled society, the outlaw had no civil rights.

Over time, outlawry faded, not just because of changes in legal codes, but also because outlaws found it increasingly difficult to evade authorities in the more densely populated urban civilization that was emerging.

On the other side of the world, the California Land Claims Act of 1851 was a major event that forced many Mexican Americans from their lands, producing a whole generation of "bandits" who fought against the expulsion. They were also called "Freedom Fighters." Most famous of these types was Joaquin Murrieta—a legend who turned from a peaceful miner into an outlaw when his land was stolen and his family attacked. Tiburcio Vasquez is another who was eventually hanged for taking the law (and other people's money) into his own hands. These guys should have been ashamed, if for nothing else than for creating the negative Mexican stereotypes that we still hold. (Think of Zorro and the Frito Bandito.)

Then there's the more extreme type of *bandido*, who is not so funny. Columbian cocaine lord Pablo Escobar comes from bandit folklore. Once considered a real life Robin Hood and a hero to an entire generation of oppressed people, Escobar eventually turned from robbing the rich and feeding the poor, to killing for his own personal gain. He became one of the worst cats in the history of criminality.

One of the most unlikely western bandits was Canadian-born Pearl Taylor (1857–1925), who came to be known as the "lady bandit." Coincidentally, she was from Lindsay, Ontario, where Wade Haines was arrested. Born to a middle-class family, she ended up as an Arizona stagecoach robber. After Pearl's release from the territorial prison in Yuma, her sister wrote a biographical play in which Pearl actually starred. It was called *The Arizona Bandit*.

There is more than one type of "beer bandit" in the overcrowded criminal marketplace. The so-called Beer Belly Bandit could give the Wade Haines story a run for its money, the culprit having committed dozens of robberies throughout Florida in the past several years. He apparently comes by his nickname honestly, thanks to his substantial girth.

In Grand Falls–Windsor, Newfoundland, the RCMP were issuing warnings in 2002 for a beer bandit of a different sort. Investigators marvelled at the audacity of the suspect, who would buy a case of beer, only to return minutes later asking for an exchange, saying he'd "bought the wrong brand." Store personnel would later find that the bottles in the returned case had been filled with water. An RCMP spokesman compared it to other scams he'd seen in other parts of the province. The scammers would buy a new pair of shoes; when they returned the box and asked for another size, the clerk would seldom if ever look to see the customer's old, worn-out shoes tucked inside. If you've got the nerve and a good sense of humour, you can get away—temporarily—with almost anything.

The Beer Bandit heist will long be regarded as a ditsy affair. But the annals of crime have many passages devoted to dumbness. A thief in Arkansas wanted beer so badly he tried throwing a cinder block through a liquor store window. But when he lifted the block and heaved it into the air, it bounced back and hit him in the head, knocking him unconscious. The attempt was futile, not just because the culprit was being videotaped, but because he'd thrown the block at Plexiglas. Lesson: cinder blocks bounce off Plexiglas.

In Ann Arbor, Michigan, a Burger King attendant informed a would-be armed robber that she couldn't open the cash drawer without him placing an order. He ordered onion rings, but walked away in frustration when the attendant informed him that onion rings weren't available for breakfast. Lesson: do your research.

And then there's the Florida bank robber who brandished a gun while wearing a ski mask and threatened the guard with the intimidating line, "Freeze mother-stickers, this is a fuck-up!" The guard broke into hysterics and the other onlookers snickered as well. Rattled by his own stupidity, the thief simply left rather than continue. One can easily imagine him drunk or stoned, relating the episode to a bunch of friends who would understand. They would all laugh about it. Lesson: if you're putting your life on the line, you've got to have a sense of humour.

Everyone agrees that the crime Wade Haines was convicted of— theft over $5,000—should not be glorified. Everyone utters this warning about "glorifying crime" while their tongues, mind you, are planted firmly in their cheeks and they're desperately trying to mask the smirks on their faces. It's hard to believe that the trial judge, no matter how forthright and dignified she is, did not at some point want to just let it all go, throw her legal briefs in the air, and laugh her head off. There is a rumour that Justice Paulette Garnett likes to dine with some regularity at the Fredericton Regent Mall Food Court—where there's a fast-food choice of New York Fries, McDonalds, Deluxe French Fries, Teriyaki Made In Japan, Manchu Wok, and Tim Hortons—so she must be pretty down-to-earth. (Note to Judge: this is playful irreverence and not a form of criminal contempt.)

So for the record, let it be said: crime does not pay. Especially this crime. There, it's been said. It's done and out of the way. And deservedly so, because after all, crime costs individuals and the system money—our hard-earned tax money. It costs Canadians to keep Wade Haines incarcerated when he should be outside driving truck and paying his income tax like a regular contributor to society. Moreover, the street-level proceeds of the beer heist, however limited the take, probably ended up contributing to the drug trade in New Brunswick. And what undoubtedly caused the whole affair in the first place was the use of cocaine and the need for more cocaine.

When you get right down to it, in fact, the Beer Bandit caper is really rooted in the madness of coke; it's a story about the direct and indirect cost of cocaine, the societal, personal, financial, and human costs of the drug. And that's nothing to glorify.

ANOTHER BIG LOAD

But for those who insisted on laughing, the Beer Bandit story has provided plenty of opportunities. Some joked that the boys holding the remainder of the stolen lager were just itching for the arrival of the spring lobster-fishing season and the chance to crack open a few thousand dozen of the luscious shellfish. This is because in May 2005, someone made off with two full truckloads of fresh lobster from the north shore of New Brunswick, valued at half a million dollars. One of the trucks was found abandoned in Montreal; the whereabouts of the other remains a mystery. Lobster and beer: a perfect summer combo.

This half-million bucks worth of misplaced crustaceans makes the seventy-thousand-dollar loss associated with the Beer Bandit heist as pale as an ale by comparison. According to the Atlantic

Provinces Trucking Association (APTA), even if there was no connection between the two jobs, the notoriety of the beer story probably encouraged the lobster heist.

The cost of trucking theft goes beyond the losses associated with out-of-service vehicles, misplaced trailers, and scoffed cargo. It's hard to believe, but the cost of truckers' insurance alone has increased as much as the price of fuel. Liability and cargo insurance typically demand multi-million-dollar coverage in this day and age. The risks and liabilities are apparently so potentially high that a niche has been carved out in the North American insurance industry. In Canada today, in spite of the fact that truckers cannot legally operate without insurance, there are only four companies who dare offer specialty insurance in this field: Markel, Kingsway, Old Republic, and Zurich. Theft is not the only basis for the immense cost of insurance. In the post-9/11 era, truckers are faced with a whole host of concerns and considerations, including the hauling of dangerous goods, protecting against terrorism, screening against the carriage of illicit cargo, and ensuring aliens are not transported to or from the United States.

There are a number of reasons for the high cost of insurance coverage. A single trailer can be carrying $15,000 worth of potatoes or hundreds of thousands of dollars worth of computers. Unless a trailer looks like a fifty-three-foot billboard, with images of Big Macs, Tim Horton's coffees, McCain French fries, or President's Choice Lasagna emblazoned across its sides, it's often hard to identify what a particular trailer is carrying. According to APTA President Ralph Boyd in Moncton, there are just so many tens of thousands of trucks on the road or parked with goods at any given moment in North America, that their identification and tracking is extremely complex.

To illustrate just how many trucks are on the road, Boyd provides some amazing facts. He says that ninety-five percent of today's North American consumables travel by truck. On a given day, depending on where you choose to take the measurement, you can see anywhere from a thousand to ten thousand trucks travelling the Trans-Canada Highway in the Maritimes. Although the APTA has several hundred members, the federal government claims there are between eighteen thousand and twenty-two thousand "carriers" in Atlantic Canada. These range from single-unit carriers, such as someone hauling raw forest products, to the big guys: three of Canada's top twenty trucking firms today are headquartered in New Brunswick alone.

The fewer the markings on a trailer, the more vulnerable the unit. Next time you're on the highway, count how many plain white or silver trailers there are. Boyd says it's easier for thieves to alter the identification and re-profile a trailer than it is an automobile. Manufacturers' components are not serialized the way auto parts are. Trailers are so common that it's hard for authorities to tell them apart. Therefore, they're harder to trace. Moreover, trucks and trailers are big, making them highly visible targets—easy marks, you could say.

"It has to do with economics," says Boyd. "Criminals focus on commodities," especially goods that are easily disposed of. This last factor did not, of course, apply very efficiently to the Spanish-labelled Moosehead beer, suggesting that perhaps the beer was not the intended target of the Beer Bandit heist. It might have been the half-million dollars worth of Crown Royal in the other Brenway trailer, which could have been fenced with much greater ease.

The Ontario Trucking Association, which like the APTA is a member of the Canadian Trucking Alliance, says that preventative action against theft is the responsibility of the industry, not law enforcement authorities. The basic principle, their published documentation says, is to make premeditated theft as difficult as possible. This calls for the adoption of best practices and for a "corporate approach" to prevention—safeguarding information about freight and its movement, and providing heightened security at terminal facilities and preventative action even on the highway. By "corporate," the association means having the people, policies, and procedures in place to stand organized against the possibility of theft and the criminal element. If the criminals are more sophisticated, which is the whole premise of organized crime, then it's the trucking industry's challenge to rise to an even higher level of sophistication. There is value even in understanding, for example, that thefts are more likely to occur on weekends and holidays.

Truckers and trucking companies today have various methods of deterring thievery, beginning with screening employees (through criminal and employment records) and encouraging those employees to keep quiet about cargoes, schedules, and movement patterns. The industry has sophisticated new allies in the hiring and identification of drivers. Layover.com, a company based in Akron, Pennsylvania, announced a partnership with DOTJobHistory.com in April 2005, which will provide trucking employers with identity authentication, a social security number validity review, address and telephone authentication, national security and narcotics watch lists, and the ability to scan criminal record databases that include more than one hundred million records for everything from traffic to criminal offences. The service not only expedites information; it provides greater assurances about authenticity. The days of accepting drivers' résumés at face value are over.

There are also the obvious measures of securing doors, electronic surveillance, parking in well-lit areas, butting trailers back to back, and parking with the rear of the unit up against fences or buildings. The most obvious on-site deterrence is the use of high chain-link fencing with barbed wire, but trucking companies are even encouraged not to store pallets, skids, and picnic tables nearby, as they could enable would-be intruders to climb over

obstructions and gain easy access to premises. Almost unbelievably, even nine months after the Beer Bandit heist, the Brenway
Transport yard in Fredericton is still as open as a public parking
lot, with free and ready access to anyone and everyone who might
care to drive in.

Beyond the technological intelligence aimed at trucking employees, the future holds the promise of other electronic systems,
some designed to disable units on the highway and others designed
to track units and their whereabouts. Vehicle location technology,
referred to as Telematics, has evolved from luxury car application
to mass-market availability. Telematics can provide wireless GPS
satellite tracking and remote control virtually anywhere cellular
service exists across North America. There was reported to be just
such a system in Wade Haines's trailer, but it was shut down by
whoever was behind the heist. One would think that these appa-
ratuses would be hidden or embedded, and thereby inaccessible
except to authorized and trained professionals, but this is apparently not the case.

The benefits of satellite tracking are vast, including "Geo Fence"
or "Geographic Border" barriers, speed and direction monitoring,
automated detection and capture of unauthorized towing, and
electronic sensing and notification of collisions. Remote control
applications are just as ingenious, including video monitoring;
remote start systems and immobilizers; the ability to track and
disable vehicle starters, ignitions, or fuel pumps; vehicle tilt sensing; and on and on. New Brunswick–based Base Engineering, for
example, sells technology internationally that enables trucking
companies to disable fuel trucks, which is particularly advanta-
geous for homeland security.

One of the biggest problems facing the trucking industry, according to Boyd, is the current capacity of police and the courts
to combat trucking theft. Except in such cases where gunpoint

hijackings occur, the norm is for trucks, trailers and goods to be stolen without harm to individuals. The relatively benign nature of these crimes—their lack of violence—has a significant effect when culprits get into court.

"If someone invades your home, it's an assault on your being," says Boyd. The same goes for armed robbery, he adds, stating that non-violent theft, where there is no physical encounter whatsoever, tends to get much lighter treatment by policing services and courts. Because of the limited resources available for police investigations of non-violent theft, the APTA encourages its members to engage the services of private investigators to help close the gap.

"The consumer pays in the end," says Boyd.

Since the earliest days of thievery, pilfering, and robbery, this has always been the case.

PART II

THE POWER OF BRAND

THE BRAND

Moosehead Breweries' official, scripted pitch—the one that appears in their brochures and on their web site—is that they don't just make a beer that you drink; it's far more syrupy and poetic than that:

It's a totally sensory experience. The touch, the sound, the sight of the unique green bottle being opened, the initial aroma of the perfect malt and hop combination as the golden lager is poured, and finally the taste, unmistakably Moosehead—clean, smooth, refreshing, premium, perfect.

There's another perspective on beer of course. Many drinkers would say that beer is just something you rent, and that the first and most frequently-repeated sensory experience from drinking beer is having to "drain the lizard"—which is highly sensory, but not exactly poetic.

Except for the part about being "clean," "smooth," and "refreshing"—of course, as a great Maritime beer, Moosehead is all of that and more—the official ad copy sounds like a *Saturday Night Live* spoof, a clear-cut case of a copywriter gone out of control. It's hard to imagine anyone being moved by this kind of flowery copy. There is, after all, a point at which the consumer's "sensory" intellect shuts down and says "get to the point," "get real," or "get lost." Which is not to say that Moosehead hasn't achieved exceptional brand heights, because it has, but through means other than sweet and sugary phrasing.

The Moosehead logo illustrates what the company calls "The King of the Forest," the majestic symbol of strength and stature—beer's MGM lion, if you will. This can't help but resonate better than the obliqueness of Coors or that beloved but disappearing Maritime favourite, Ten-Penny (which is, incidentally, a Moosehead Breweries product). The best-known and most-loved beer brands tend to be associated with historic famous people (Ontario's John Labatt, Nova Scotia's Alexander Keith, Boston's Sam Adams) or beasts (the moose, Anheuser-Busch's famous Clydesdales, Newfoundland's Black Horse).

Moosehead is the public face of the beer, but behind the brand there's the Oland family, descendants of a clan that originally came from Sweden, where the family originated as sea captains and sailors more than four hundred years ago. Around 1600, as the story goes, two Swedish Olands settled in Bristol, England, where one was killed in a riot while serving as mayor, and the other married an English girl. Three generations later, John James Dunn Oland was born in 1819. In 1842, he married Susannah Culverwell, who introduced him to English country traditions.

John and Susannah settled on an English estate. He attended Cambridge University and later joined the accounting staff of the London and Southwestern Railway, which led to an engagement with the Intercontinental Railway, a company that was involved with new railway developments in Nova Scotia. John, Susannah, and their seven children sailed from England on the barque *Spirit of the Queen* on March 21, 1865, arriving in Halifax one month later. After a brief period residing in Windsor, they moved to Dartmouth. It was in an area behind their Dartmouth home where Susannah taught her sons to brew the mixture of barley malt, hops and yeast for a brown October ale of the type brewed on their estate in England. A pair of investors brought about the founding of the first Oland brewery. Scroll ahead to 1870 and the untimely death of John after falling from his horse, and we find Susannah and sons even more intent on making lager, ale, and stout. An inheritance from England iced the cake, allowing her to buy a controlling interest in the now-thriving business under the name S. Oland Sons and Co. Eight years later, disaster struck in the form of a fire, but the Olands were not to be outdone. The family rebuilt and prospered. Susannah Oland died in 1886, a month after her sixty-eighth birthday.

Eventually, after numerous developments and crises, the Olands built a brewery in Saint John, New Brunswick. The family tree branches out to Derek Oland, son of the late Moosehead patriarch, Philip W. Oland. Derek is current CEO, with sons Patrick and Andrew in the wings, maintaining the traditions of Canada's oldest independent brewery.

It's quite a transition from the staid Oland family to the contemporary street-level branding of Moosehead products, the names of which are familiar to every Maritimer. The current list of Oland brands includes Moosehead Ale, Moosehead Lager, Moosehead Light, Moosehead Premium Dry, Moosehead Dry Ice, Clancy's Amber, Alpine, Alpine Light, and of course, the stalwart Ten-Penny.

Moosehead has gone through a number of advertising slogans over the years: "It's In Your Nature"; "Aah, the Wilderness"; "Heed the Call!"; "The Taste of Independence"; "Live Big"; "Bigger is Better"; "Refreshingly Independent"; "The World Enjoys Our Lager"; and the line that was repeated endlessly during the Beer Bandit caper, "The Moose Is Loose." There's also another slogan, rarely seen in the Maritimes, but used in some markets: the irresistibly naughty "Nice Rack." One can only imagine the reaction of matriarch Susannah, no doubt a lady of some refinement, if the slogan were explained to her. But, hey, it is the highly competitive beer business, after all, a sector ripe with "tits and ass" and sex and freedom and nightlife and independence. Moosehead is far from alone in recognizing that sometimes sex does sell. And as some agency type might rationalize, "Are you prepared to argue that the moose does not have a nice rack?"

THE PR GUYS

What do you do when you wake up one normal August morning, tool down to the office, grab your morning coffee, settle in for a day's work, open your e-mail, and suddenly discover that fate has handed you the most lucrative product promotion of your career, probably the most lucrative product promotion in the history of your company, with no apparent strings attached? You do exactly what Joel Levesque did when he received such an e-mail on the morning of August 18, 2004.

As Moosehead's vice president of public affairs, Levesque is responsible for the company's community and government relations, external and internal communications, corporate charitable donations programs and other marketing communications support efforts. Middle-aged Levesque is youthfully trim, well turned out, and personable. He has been around PR circles in New Brunswick for three decades, working at different times for a regulated monopoly, for a civic government, and as a vice president with a large regional communications firm. He's received the Bronze Anvil award from the New York–based Public Relations Society of America, and he was appointed to the Canadian Public Relations Society College of Fellows. His vast experience teaches him how to communicate while simultaneously examining what he's saying and how you're reacting, anticipating what's to be asked next. This allows him to measure how far he can go with facts, beliefs and embellishments. He has a discreet but open style. He's what you might call a "mature PR practitioner," or more casually, a "true PR guy."

After absorbing the e-mail from Moosehead's Bruce Robinson, which related the story of the beer heist, Levesque was on the phone to his Toronto-based public relations contractor faster than you can say "Guadalajara." The object of his speed dial was Ciris Public Relations president Jeff Lake, a native New Brunswicker and former city editor at the Fredericton *Daily Gleaner*. They discussed the pros and cons of Moosehead Breweries pro-actively issuing a news release.

As Levesque tells it, "I said, 'Jeff, look, here's the story,' and he agreed with me that it was probably worth the effort, with no foreseeable down side. We had to be careful because at that point, we didn't know if the driver was involved or not, so we didn't want to be too flip about it.

"We had looked at the upside and the downside," explains Levesque, "examining the question: 'Is there any negative consequence to issuing this?' We discussed the pros and cons and we just figured, 'well, we'll issue a release.' Within an hour of getting that e-mail, I had a release and had distributed it locally to the New Brunswick media. A standard PR strategy is to control the message, so we were out there first."

Lake says that on the first day of the story, his big concern was "that we had so little to go on. We didn't know what had happened to the driver, so we had to be cautious. For us as much as anything, it was a case of disbelief."

While Levesque and Lake had been constantly examining the possible consequences of their corporate news release, the RCMP were busily taking stock of the situation and trying to determine whether Wade Haines was alive or dead. Several hours later, the Oromocto District 2 detachment of the RCMP issued that initial news release of their own, announcing the missing truckload of beer and their search for Wade Haines.

As Moosehead and the Mounties were issuing their respective media releases, Wade Haines was travelling sleepily somewhere between Grand Falls and Lindsay, where, by that time, he must have been pondering that age-old question: "What the hell was I thinking?"

The Beer Bandit caper was an out-of-control *fiesta* of coverage from the minute Levesque and his associates made the decision to issue their press release. What followed, of course, was astonishing: pica after pica, inch after inch, headline after headline of legitimate hard news copy—free! Broadcast upon broadcast from every TV and radio station in the land—free! Tongue-in-cheek editorializing from everyone with a medium to speak through—free! It was all a free ride!

"I liken what happened to making a snowball and setting it rolling at the top of a hill," says Levesque. "I figured by the time it got to the bottom of the hill, it would be a bigger snowball."

Instead, it turned into an avalanche.

In the face of an ordeal that seemed—as Canadian Press writer Chris Morris described it—"more and more like a Superbowl commercial," Levesque and his PR colleagues were faced with the daily challenge of keeping pace with media requests, keeping track of the exposure, and along the way, continuing to exercise good taste. It was still, after all, a serious crime.

The consumer impressions that the beer bandit story drew— each impression being a single person's exposure to a print or electronic media story—grew into the tens of millions.

"I mean, CNN used it one day, scrolling across the bottom of the screen for the full day," says Levesque. It was during the network's extensive hurricane coverage, so the audience was huge and highly attentive. It's fair to say that Canadian stories of any sort are an extreme rarity on national US media, so this level of exposure was quite unexpected. People kept calling Levesque saying they'd seen the story on Ted Turner's trend-setting network.

"So we had started the snowball down the hill and the media started calling," recalls Levesque. "Then we started doing, of course, all of the right things. We took a colour photo of the can of Moosehead beer and sent it off to the media. The next day on the front pages of newspapers right across the country, there was the imagery of our brand."

People who didn't go beyond the headline, people who didn't even read the story, were still left with the subliminal consumer impression of the Moosehead can. "Consumer impressions" are the brass ring of every brand marketer in the world—it's what they dream about at night. And here the Moosehead people were experiencing a marketer's dream come true, over and over and over again.

The media then began lining up, asking to come into the Moosehead production plant in Saint John to videotape the inner workings of production, which is standard stuff for visual filler on television. Levesque, being the PR pro that he is, being the popular lecturer on public relations and public affairs management that he is, already had good quality B-roll on hand. B-roll is generic stock footage of the production facility and the product, which is available for media use, making a television reporter's or producer's job that much easier. But Levesque went a step further, creating new B-roll of the Spanish cans. "All of the networks were asking to come in," he says, "but because I already had it, I was able to say, 'Here it is.' You can't buy that."

Levesque had spoken to RCMP spokesman Gary Cameron, who tried to relate to him the number of thefts in New Brunswick during an average day, week, or year. By his rough estimate, the Beer Bandit story had received more coverage, in just a couple of days, than an entire year's worth of New Brunswick crime stories. Not all of this was necessarily by accident. Nothing was fabricated, but the way the story was presented certainly couldn't have hurt its grab on the media. For starters, there was the issue of money.

"We gave the retail value of the shipment," explains Levesque. "If the beer was sold in New Brunswick, it would be worth $75,000. Then [there was] the question of how much beer was on the trailer."

At the brewery, Moosehead employees always measure and refer to beer in cases. Each case contains twenty-four cans of beer. Levesque knew that saying there were 2,100 cases of beer on the truck wouldn't really sound like a lot of product to the layperson. Even if you said that the shipment was 4,200 dozen, it still didn't sound like such a huge deal. But when you multiply that by twelve, suddenly it's 50,400 cans of beer.

"Well," says Levesque nine months after the heist, "50,400 became the gospel. That's the number that's still quoted to this day." It was a number that ordinary people seized on because their consumer sensibility suddenly grasped the magnitude of the theft.

After the initial rush of media interest, Levesque and Lake figured things would die down. But uncharacteristically, the snowball just kept on growing. As the story unfolded over the next few weeks, "a lot of serendipitous things" happened, as Levesqe puts it. "A couple of cans were found. Well, that became a story. And then more cans were found, and so it became evident that every time in the next week or so that cans would be found, then that would also become a part of the story."

Then crazy incidents really started popping up. Every manic twist in the story created the irresistible temptation to go wild, or at least to have a good laugh. However, Levesque's determination to keep a straight face during dozens of media inquiries, in spite of all the wacky new story angles that kept emerging, speaks volumes about his professionalism. It was a constant balancing act in the face of editorials that relentlessly made light of the story.

For example, the company had to temper its reaction when four pallets of the beer were found strewn across a ditch on a remote country road, the result of a flatbed trailer becoming unhitched from a scurrying half-ton and careening into Owen Lawson's farm field. When police were led to a stash of the cans found at a marijuana growing operation near Doaktown, a friendly little community along the Miramichi River, they discovered that a handful of the cans had been mauled, and the contents presumably consumed, by one or more black bears. Even Levesque couldn't resist cracking a joke about that one: "The thing that really impressed us is the bears chose the Moosehead beer over the dope," he's quoted as saying. After such a prolonged onslaught, how could you blame him? Media folks, meanwhile, without Levesque's prodding, were conjuring images of bears staggering around the backwoods of New Brunswick drunk on lager and stoned on grass.

Levesque claims that after thirty years as a public relations professional, he's never run across anything quite like the Beer

Bandit affair. "I've been involved in many, many major stories," he says. "Funny stories, serious stories, business stories, government stories." He includes on this list the Saint John oil refinery explosion when he worked for Irving, the good and bad news about the Canadian navy frigate program, and the more recent controversy over the New Brunswick government's decision to subsdize the construction of a Molson brewery right in Moosehead's own backyard. In the spring of 1986, on his first day on the job with the City of Saint John, Levesque walked into the story of a gas leak in the city sewer system and the ensuing explosion that affected numerous downtown buildings. "We've created stories and been involved in stories, but we've never, ever been involved in anything like this, that had just taken off."

Toronto PR guy Lake says that in a twenty-six-year career with several national public relations and communications firms, only one story has even come close to that of the Beer Bandit heist: the controversy surrounding *Sports Illustrated*'s refusal to run an Adidas advertisement that suggested, but didn't really show, the genitals of a team of naked soccer players. The *Sports Illustrated* piece might have been a bigger story for its brief moment in time, "but nothing has ever lasted so long" as the Beer Bandit story, says Lake. One reason, he believes, is that the heist occurred during a typically dry, mid-August news period. Another is that everyone involved with the story communicated with everyone else.

"The RCMP," says Lake, "were exceptionally good at communications. Also, the story lent itself to tremendous PR coverage because it showcased how the police solve a crime."

"It's a funny story," says Levesque. "It truly is a funny story that captured people's imagination. As I've said many times to the media, it's kind of like every college boy's dream to find a pallet full of beer."

The more evident it became to Levesque and Lake that the beer heist story "had legs," the greater was their challenge to capitalize on the occurrence while keeping things in good taste—not letting Moosehead's involvement seem too purposeful. They didn't have too much to worry about, because eventually the story itself *became* the story. The media began calling asking, "How much publicity has this generated? What's the value of the publicity? You must be thrilled with the free publicity."

"In fact," says Levesque, "some media stopped using the word 'Moosehead' because I think they were feeling it was being overused. You'll find some media who after a week or so stopped saying 'Moosehead beer.' They'd just say 'beer.'"

Levesque uses the long-running CBC radio program *As It Happens* as a prime example of how the story broke through otherwise inaccessible media forms. The tremendously popular primetime interview show did not just one, but two stories on the heist. "I've pitched many stories over the years to *As It Happens* but this is the first one that got picked up," he says.

There was yet another indication that perhaps Moosehead should try to keep certain aspects of the story alive. Consumers started calling and offering their own suggestions for Beer Bandit promotions, Beer Bandit commercials, Beer Bandit web sites, and even Beer Bandit video games. "We were being inundated with consumers and others who wanted to do things," claims Levesque.

Then the T-shirt idea came along. It seemed like a benign thing, especially compared to some of the other, wilder proposals the brewery had received. Hudson Design in Moncton was charged with creating a T-shirt concept. Hudson's Maurice Belliveau came back with a winning premise: a design that looked like a souvenir shirt from a rock group's concert tour. The shirt showed a Spanish-labelled can of Moosehead and a list of all the places where the beer was found. The tour dates for Toronto and Mexico were crossed off as "Cancelled."

"I made two phone calls," recalls Levesque, "one to the *T-J* [the Saint John *Telegraph-Journal*] and one to CBC and said: 'Look, you might be interested. We're doing this T-shirt.' Well, boom!" In the ensuing exposure, the assignment editor at ATV sent reporter Mike Cameron up to the Moosehead store in Saint John. "Mike turns to me, shakes his head, and says, 'You know, I can't believe this is my fourth trip over here on this story. I can't believe I'm doing this again! I can't believe I'm doing this story again!'"

As Levesque tells it, the *Telegraph-Journal* sent a photographer over and had a clerk in the Moosehead store pose with the shirt held high. Wham! The next morning, there it was in a full-colour, front-page photo. The T-shirt took off like mad. At first, Moosehead ordered five hundred shirts, which were gone within days. So they ordered another five hundred. All told, more than five thousand shirts were moved through the Saint John store alone (which is not exactly conveniently situated), backed by a presence on the merchandising section of the Moosehead Breweries web site.

"People were buying, not one, not two, but they were buying, four, five, eight," says Levesque. "People were coming here and buying them and they were sending them to their family members all over the country because people had heard about the story." Even the T-shirt was not enough. People wanted the shirt, but they also wanted press clippings to send along with the shirt. "So we were making press clippings, so that people could send them to their grandchildren in Calgary."

Levesque maintains that if the company had really wanted to push the T-shirts out the door, they could have sold another five thousand units or more. He adds that net proceeds from the sale of the T-shirt were provided to the food bank in Oromocto, based on the recommendation of the RCMP, whose investigating team for the crime is based there.

Levesque agrees with Jeff Lake's comments about the investigating police. "I can't say enough good about them. They were in constant communication with us, in terms of what was going on in the investigation, both asking for our help but also just keeping us informed. Our concern from day one was that we didn't want to encourage more truck hijackings, and that's one of the reasons we ended up doing a victim impact statement," which the company submitted to Justice Paulette Garnett at the conclusion of Haines's February 2005 trial. Both Moosehead and the RCMP were in the same mindset. Moosehead even supplied photographic images for the Mounties' web site.

Levesque explains: "They'll tell you about the amount of traffic that this story generated to their web site and the volume has stayed up. I thought they were extremely professional and put a lot of time and effort into the investigation. And, well, they got their man. It was a successful prosecution and we're pleased that he [Haines] was found guilty."

Even after the T-shirt, the story lived on, says Levesque. "People have kept saying to me, with the coverage of the trial and the sentencing, they said: 'That's got to be it.' But I said that the way the story was going, I'm sure we have not heard the end of this story. I said the snow is going to melt and someone is going to find another pallet of beer, or there's going to be some other twist or turn."

The next thing you know, someone would want to do a book, says Levesque. As if.

The Mexican Connection

Gerardo Arturo Rodriguez Campollo is a Guatemalan national who landed a job at the Soriana food store chain after earning his MBA at Thunderbird University in Phoenix, Arizona, and a stint working at Oracle in Washington, DC. The visa restrictions imposed after 9/11 got in the way of his staying stateside, which resulted in his relocating to Mexico. He may be only twenty-five years old, but he knows the ropes of Mexican retail, and he knows how to cut a deal. Until January 2005, he was responsible at Soriana for the import purchasing of wines, spirits, beers, and other non-food products. He's now moved into canned vegetables, dressings, and sauces, but he was on the scene when Moosehead made its first foray in the Mexican market, and he recalls the move very vividly. His official title is *Compras Importaciones y Marca Propia*, or Imports and Private Label Buyer.

Soriana, says Campollo, broke the retail beer market wide open and initiated a trend when they started selling Moosehead at lower prices and targeting the blue-collar crowd. (Another foreign beer, Heineken, was aimed at the white-collar class.) In December 2002, Moosehead's first month in Mexico, seventy truckloads of Moosehead Lager, each one carrying 8800 six-packs, rolled into Soriana's central shipping depots. Do your own math. Before that intervention, a six-pack of beer in what would become Moosehead's class cost thirty-nine or forty pesos. Moosehead was launched at twenty-six pesos and the market went nuts.

"People went crazy," says Campollo. He recalls seeing people carrying six thousand pesos' worth of Moosehead out the door at a time, like they were carrying a pallet of the stuff. "This is not a normal thing," he says. In Juárez, for example, where Campollo visited a string of Soriana stores and where people are known for their consumption of beer, the right combination of price, quality, taste, and lifestyle marketing drove sales through the roof. Like at home in Canada, Moosehead's promotional aids didn't hurt. The company sent along point-of-purchase materials, including posters depicting hot Canadian-looking girls on a sandy beach. And there were coolers and chalkboards, whose "handwritten" pricing added a sense of urgency to the value being offered.

"We were really shocked," he says, when Moosehead hit the level of seventy percent of Soriana's beer sales, beating even the home-grown favorite Corona. Considering that supermarket chains account for twenty to thirty percent of all beer sales in the country of Mexico, a lot of volume is at stake in such beer wars.

"Both major breweries in Mexico started getting alarmed," and decided they'd better get on the deals-and-special-offers band-wagon, explains Campollo.

If the volume of Moosehead sales was extraordinary, it was equally unusual for a shipment of Canadian beer destined for Mexico to go missing, at least on the north side of the border. Campollo first heard about the missing beer from suppliers who'd seen and heard about the heist on CNN. He immediately checked CNN.com and couldn't believe what he was reading.

Enter Moosehead's VP of international sales, Bruce Robinson, who confirms that Soriana stores are true "hypermarkets," a European term for a hybrid retailer that looks like a grocery store, a Wal-Mart, and a Costco all at the same time. In other words, it's the kind of place where you can buy cereal, beer, and a motorcycle in one stop. To put the scale of these hypermarkets in perspective, consider that a typical Soriana store has thirty checkout counters and is four times the size of an Atlantic Canadian Sobeys, which might have a dozen or so checkouts. There are even bigger hypermakrets in Brazil that have up to a hundred checkout lanes. (One can only wonder whether their aisles are any wider than ours, and whether or not people move any faster when they're frustratingly lodged in front of your cart, staring at tins of peas or brownie mix.)

"They are *the* guys," says Robinson, referring to Soriana's number two position in the Mexican retail marketplace, second only to Wal-Mart, over whom they're "even further advanced in some respects." Soriana was featured as a success story in a recent edition of *Fortune* magazine as the number two but coming-on-strong retail chain in Mexico.

Being the globetrotting Moosehead sales chief that he is, Robinson hooked up with Soriana at Anuga, the world's largest food exposition, held every two years in Cologne, Germany. At the time, the expansive chain just happened to be looking for a new imported beer product. In a country where there are "hundreds of imported beers," it's an amazing feat that Moosehead was able to break through the clutter.

Hundreds?

"Yes, hundreds," says Robinson.

Robinson came to Moosehead eight years ago after a stint at Labatt's in Toronto. He and the rest of the company's export sales team are responsible for continuing relationships that make Moosehead available in some twenty different countries, including the United States, New Zealand, Austraila, Ireland, England, France, Germany, Switzerland, Chile, Japan, Panama, Iceland, Malaysia, South Korea, the Netherlands, the Dominican Republic, and for a while, Thailand. (What? No Moosehead in Swaziland?) Exporting to so many countries is a complicated affair, as many countries, including Mexico, have very stringent laws governing packaging. In Mexico, the obvious provision is for Spanish labelling.

🫎 🫎 🫎

Ultimately, the availability of Moosehead Lager in Mexico, even if it is limited to Soriana food stores, is due to the North American Free Trade Agreement, that fuzzy maze of an accord that few people truly understand. Most folks have only a basic grasp of the main effect of NAFTA: that goods will flow in a less restricted manner across US, Mexican, and Canadian borders. The cross-border beer trade hasn't attracted very much attention, mostly because beer is not a staple like wood or beef, and because it hasn't resonated strongly with any US lobby group with the power to influence Congress—yet.

Robinson says that before the free trade agreement, Mexico was a hard case for importing. It was a "very closed country," he says, especially when it came to the movement of alcohol across its borders. After NAFTA came into being in 1994, change began trickling into effect. "Not everything associated with NAFTA happened the following day," says Robinson.

It's also hard to break into Mexico because the country produces a lot of its own high-quality beers, principally through the two major breweries, Grupo Modelo and Femsa. But international access to the market shifted three or four years ago when the two majors were partially taken over by the foreign conglomerates Anheuser-Busch and Interbrew (the latter of which is itself now part of an even larger conglomerate called InBev). The emerging presence of those two international players changed the climate for doing beer business in Mexico—forever.

Although export markets tend to bob and weave and shift according to world events and the state of currencies, there is something to be said for import receptiveness in countries that have a natural affinity for Canada. Robinson says that whether its beer or blueberries, fish or bottled water, Canada's image doesn't hurt when negotiating in certain jurisdictions. These would include European countries, and happily, Mexico.

There is a degree of irony, though, with this crafty NAFTA. Think about the fact that northbound Mexican truckers carrying trailer-loads of Sol, and southbound Canadian truckers carrying Moosehead, can wave as they pass each other on the US Interstate system. A decade after the free-trade agreement went into effect, Mexican beer brands such as Sol and Corona are doing well in Canada, and are doing even better in the United States, thanks mostly to the burgeoning Latino population there. The great "sucking sound" predicted by one-time US presidential candidate and free-trade opponent Ross Perot turns out to be the sound not only of American jobs going south of the border, but also of American and Canadian consumers literally sucking back the most popular brands of Mexican beer. Many say this is at the expense of domestic brands.

For Canadians, there is also that intangible, irrational style thing: the silly, trendy exoticism of stuffing wedges of lime (which Mexicans apparently do not bother with) into the tops of clear bottles of Corona. In fact, in Canada and the US, everything about beer is about imagery and how consumers see their lifestyles. Mexican beers like Corona evoke Madison Avenue images of beautiful, sun-tanned people drinking light-bodied pale lagers on the shores of beautiful Gulf of Mexico sand, throwing their cell phones into the surf when the idyllic setting is broken by an unwanted ring. The Mexicans' interest in the Moosehead brand, on the other hand, has less to do with exoticism and is more simply rooted in good taste and price. The taste is easy to understand, but it's a wonder, really, when you stop and think about it, how Moosehead beer can be sold so inexpensively when it has to travel so far to get there.

PART III

THE SUPPORTING CAST

THE FARMER

Owen Lawson is a stout man, a suitable guy to find manoeuvring a tractor and splitting wood in a clearing near his remote farm in East Newbridge, north of Woodstock, New Brunswick. It's so remote, as a neighbour put it, "it's where the electricity ends."

Lawson is sixty-two years of age but still boasts a boyish-looking face. He wears the predictable farmer hat, which when removed reveals a hairless scalp. There are permanent circular lines where the hat ends and his forehead and Mike Tyson–like neck begin. You could mistake Lawson's robustness for a byproduct of beer consumption, but he says otherwise: it's just the kind of build and girth that come from eating meat and potatoes and doing good, honest, hard farm labour.

Lawson owns 485 acres, located twenty minutes from the bridge that spans the St. John River at Woodstock. Route 585 grows more rural the farther you go, through sprawling tracts of birch trees, marshes, and farms. The road travels past Lawson's white house and barnyard—a succession of structures built over time—but God knows where it goes. And the polite neighbours are right: after Lawson's place, there is no more electrical power. Beyond that, you're in Unabomber country.

When I arrived at Lawson's farm to conduct an interview, there were two dogs in Lawson's yard, which immediately made me apprehensive. The presence of tag-team rural canines makes one think twice about getting out of the car, but this pair was happy just to snooze the afternoon away undisturbed and unruffled. It must have been their way of mentally blocking out the overwhelming presence of horse flies. After successive, unanswered knocks at the door and a few beeps of the horn, I undertook a search of the back forty. At the end of a potholed logging road unfit for my Camry, I found Lawson earning his bread and butter.

"I do a little beef farming," he explains. "I keep pigs, cattle and I raise a little hay, work in the woods in the winter."

It's lonely work that is not without its dangers. Several years ago, he was working alone in a nearby field when he got caught in a combine and nearly lost his life. His shirt got snagged in an auger. His voice breaks slightly as he describes how close he came to buying the farm, so to speak: "It kinda tore me up considerably. I whooped and hollered and tried to get out of the thing. I'd figured that was it, boys. A fellow heard me hollering. He went out to get a cucumber in his garden, the guy next door. And he came over and shut the combine off. It was just a fluke. The combine was still idling."

When he got out of it, all he had on was his shoes, a kerchief on his neck, and one sleeve of his shirt. And that was it. "She just chewed me right from there to there just like hamburger," he says, motioning up and down the length of his body. Miraculously, there was no need for an operation. "They just patched me up."

By comparison, his connection to the Moosehead beer heist seems minor.

"You kinda don't sweat the little stuff," Lawson says.

But neither will he forget what took place that afternoon at his farm. Like everyone else who owns a television, Lawson was no stranger to the story, having heard about it a few days earlier. But aware as he was, in the quiet workaday vacuum of East Newbridge, he was completely unprepared for his involuntary induction into the Beer Bandit story.

"I was loading the silage wrapper on the truck there," he recalls. "I was taking it to another fellow there in Millville. This half-ton with this trailer behind it rolled by and I was just getting out of [my] half-ton, went to jump up on the tractor to load it on, eh."

Lawson says he can't be sure, but he thinks the truck was an older Ford, tarnished and faded enough that its colour was unremarkable.

Lawson turned for the slightest moment and mounted the tractor to hoist the silage wrapper. When he casually looked back, he noticed that something about the half-ton and its carriage had changed, that it didn't look quite the same as it passed into the distance. "I noticed him the second time going up the road and there was no trailer behind the truck. I said, 'Boys, he must be stupid because it must have unhooked.' I was sure there was a trailer on it when it went by there, just out of the corner of my eye. The truck was right opposite the gate you see when he went by."

He wouldn't have been more than two hundred feet from the truck and trailer when it whizzed by. "I just presumed it was a load of lumber or something," he says. "It was covered up with a blue tarp and he whistled along, just going about thirty miles an hour, just going along slow. Then I jumped up on the tractor and then I could see the half ton going on up beyond a big bunch of weeds and machinery piled there and he didn't have any trailer behind him. I said, 'Jeez, that's funny.' I had the tractor running so I couldn't hear anything. I imagine you could have heard the trailer crashing, but not with the tractor running. So I went on and I loaded my ma-

Moosehead ad created by Jim McVicar,
Media Planet, Saint John, New Brunswick.

Now available in more secure,
50,000-can packs

T-shirt design, Hudson Design Group, Moncton, New Brunswick.

BEER HEIST TOUR 04

MAY BE COMING TO A TOWN NEAR YOU!

- TORONTO AUGUST 16 CANCELLED!
- GRAND FALLS AUGUST 17 240 CANS
- MEXICO AUGUST 19 CANCELLED!
- FREDERICTON AUGUST 19 2 CANS
- WOODSTOCK AUGUST 24 6,560 CANS
- NACKAWIC AUGUST 25 1,322 CANS
- NACKAWIC AUGUST 30 300 CANS
- MILLVILLE AUGUST 31 5,000 CANS
- PENNIAC SEPTEMBER 6 200 CANS

¿DONDE ESTÁ MI CERVEZA?

Michael de Adder,
the Moncton *Times & Transcript*

Michael de Adder,
the Moncton *Times & Transcript*

Michael de Adder,
the Moncton *Times & Transcript*

Michael de Adder,
the Moncton *Times & Transcript*

THE BEER BANDIT CAPER

Wade Haines with mentor George Piers, manager
of the Fredericton Community Kitchen, August 5, 2005.

Stephen MacGillivray

chine. I suppose it took me fifteen, twenty minutes, I'm not sure. And then I got curious. I said, 'Jeez, I better go look. I know there was a trailer there behind that tractor when it went by.'"

Lawson ventured out to the road where he found a huge scrape mark. There, poking out of the ditch, was the trailer, with four smashed wooden pallets and beer cans sprinkled all over Lawson's land. "A good percentage of it I'd say was broken," says Lawson. "Them little cans aren't very thick. They're not like a can of soup." And there were a lot of cans. "I have no idea where they were going or where they'd come from. And they never came back to look for anything. I looked it over there and I said, 'Jeez, that looks like Spanish. You know it don't look like the English I know, so it must be Spanish beer.'"

The next thing Lawson knew, neighbours were arriving to stop, look and take pictures. "Oh, it was a big deal," he says.

A neighbour came over and he and Lawson chatted about what to do. "We talked there and I said, 'Gee, I suppose we have to report that. That must be the stuff.' So we reported it and a Mountie came out and looked it over and then they proceeded to try and find the guy."

Regarding his appearance in court, Lawson says it was no big deal. He couldn't tell them any more than what he'd told them in his police interview, so he just went about it naturally. But Lawson had one of the most cherished lines of the trial when he told the judge he was glad his bull didn't get into the stash—glad because Jock the bull weighs over a ton. He's a Saler breed, not your average cow, and not easy to round back up when he's sober. Lawson's never seen Jock in a drunken state and wouldn't care to.

Lawson talks as though he enjoyed some of the attention. "A girl I went to school with [and who now lives] in Florida called me and said she'd seen me on the news. I hadn't heard tell of her for forty years. It was CNN or I don't know what she'd seen it on down there. I've got relatives over in Maine and they all called and said, 'Gee, we saw you on television last night.' Now, I missed it. I was working."

Regarding Haines, Lawson was ambivalent. "I saw him in court. He looked like a fine gentleman. I guess maybe he did it. I don't know. I couldn't see where they had a lot of evidence really against him." Haines might have preferred to have Lawson in the jury box rather than on the witness stand.

"It was the talk of the town I guess," says Lawson, reflecting on his moment in the limelight. Except that East Newbridge is not a town. It's just where the electricity ends.

THE BEARS

On October 19, 2004, a guy walked into the Blackville district office of the RCMP with a single can of Spanish-labelled Moosehead and a story about a marijuana grow site.

Blackville is a logging and sawmill community where the Miramichi River runs gently by and where the legend of the Dungarvon Whooper—the shrieking ghost of a murdered lumber-camp cook—lives on. It's just a quiet little section of woods, but with a legend that plays tricks with the mind.

Sgt. Paul Brown and his twenty-odd station members constitute the smallest RCMP detachment in New Brunswick, yet they're responsible for one of the largest coverage areas. Nearly all of it is rural. The zone runs from McGivney to the Heath steel mines, covering half of the Plaster Rock Highway, down to Doaktown, and all areas in between. If you're unfamiliar with these parts of New Brunswick, it's kind of like Tora Bora in Afghanistan—lots and lots of territory, but very little settlement or civilization.

"Rural New Brunswick," says thirty-five-year-old Brown in

a moment of understatement, "is so rural." And being from Mactaquac, New Brunswick, Brown is something of an authority on what constitutes "rural."

Two members of Brown's detachment were sent to the site of the beer find, forty-four kilometres from Blackville on what is known as the Office Road, which is off the Semi-Wagon Road. This is hardcore logging-road country, where mosquitoes soar like condors and black flies get their three square meals dining on lumberjacks, salmon anglers, and animals.

"We definitely didn't know what we had," says Sgt. Brown, referring to the presentation of the single can of Moosehead and the report of the Marijuana grow op. Once there, the officers found what Brown describes as a typical abandoned grow site: drying tables, propane tanks, tents, coolers, cots, and chairs—"the disposable assets" of the trade. Grow sites such as this, in spite of their elaborate set-ups, are nearly impossible to locate from the ground because of that heavy-duty rural-ness. The RCMP sometimes use aircraft to search for culprits and their illegal activities, but even detection from the air is difficult because of the vastness of the land.

A frost had killed off what remained of the marijuana, a pretty typical occurrence for that time of year, but the seasonal change in temperature did manage to keep the one hundred and fourteen cans of Moosehead found at the site nicely chilled. Amid the heap of intact suds were half a dozen cans which had been emptied and which exhibited very distinctive tooth impressions. By the mangled markings on the cans, it was evident to Brown and his investigating officers that they'd come across a black-bear happy hour.

"How ironic was it that they'd sold the beer off to individuals involved in the illegal drug trade," says Brown, suggesting that the beer heist just had to have been linked in some way to the marijuana growers, and quite possibly to a broader crime circuit.

Finding the beer amid the marijuana grow op was one thing, but the bear angle was a journalistic clincher. Every editorial cartoonist and media person between Halifax and Ballahack was on the case yet again.

On October 20, 2004, the Blackville RCMP issued the following media release:

200 stolen Moosehead beer cans discovered at marijuana production site
Doaktown, NB—The RCMP in District 6 Miramichi have discovered close to 200 Spanish labelled Moosehead beer cans which were stolen from a shipment of 50,000 cans in August, thanks to a tip from the public.

The cans were discovered at a well hidden marijuana production site on October 19, 2004 in the woods, 25 miles off the Acadian Road near Doaktown, NB. In addition to the beer cans, the police discovered thousands of dollars in equipment which would be used for marijuana production, including two camouflaged tents.

The police believe the marijuana was grown elsewhere and brought to this location for production.

The police were able to recover 114 of the beer cans intact because many were emptied or destroyed. Six of the cans were discovered with bite marks in them, indicating a bear had at one point been into the beer.

The RCMP is continuing to investigate.

"Once I did the media release," says Brown, "the calls were just incredible."

He explains that when he does a typical news clip about a crime or a missing person or what have you, "it's something you never think about," but when news has real legs, it can carry far and wide.

He got calls from friends and former RCMP comrades from across the country.

Of his thirteen years in the force, Sgt. Brown says he'd "definitely run into odd things before," but nothing like the Beer Bandit caper. Of the humour behind the entire episode, Brown says, "You might as well laugh as cry," affirming that in spite of the magnitude of the crime, it is undeniably a funny story.

THE PROSECUTOR

On average, there are fifty thousand court cases per year in New Brunswick, five thousand in the Fredericton jurisdiction alone. Province wide, eighty-five percent of the caseload is criminal in nature (as opposed to motor vehicle infractions and the like). Eighty percent of those criminal cases never go to trial, either because of guilty pleas or lack of evidence. There are five criminal prosecutors in the New Brunswick capital's justice division, one of whom was Beer Bandit trial lead Cameron Gunn, a lawyer with more than ten years of criminal prosecutions under his belt.

Gunn is a youthful, well-attired, dark-haired, robust figure who works as a lawyer but aspires to be a writer; his fictional creation is a detective named Hamnet Davidson, whose first whodunit is set in St. Andrews by the Sea. Gunn has an intriguing idea for a non-fiction book as well: *Stumbling In The Footsteps of Franklin: How to Lead a (Slightly) Prosperous and (Somewhat) Successful Life*. The book is a satirical self-help project based on Benjamin Franklin's thirteen virtues. The writing thing adds an edge to Gunn's role in the case. Like any writer, he's always looking for unusual hooks and plots. And like any prosecutor, he's come to learn that truth is stranger than fiction.

Like his defence counterpart, Ron "the Cat" Morris, Gunn is a Miramichi native. "I've been a Moosehead drinker from way back," he says, even though Miramichi is "the land of Alpine people." Morris, on the other hand, is a rum drinker. Gunn says he and Morris have a similar courtroom style and a good working relationship.

According to Gunn, the two have met in court on dozens and dozens of cases over the years, but the Beer Bandit case was their first jury trial together. Statistics explain why, he says, as ninety-eight percent of trials are by judge, not by jury. He adds that there are usually fewer than fifty jury trials in New Brunswick in any given year, even though murder charges require jury trials.

Gunn says he was confident about the Beer Bandit case because Haines's story just didn't add up, and because Pierre Gervais and the RCMP colleagues were "dogged" on the case. He says the police made his job as prosecutor a lot easier by being thorough and by being receptive to his ideas. Despite the lack of direct evidence linking Haines to the theft, Gunn says the Mounties were successful in accumulating more than enough good circumstantial evidence.

"He [Haines] told police things that just couldn't have been true," says Gunn. "His own story certainly did not help him." This is the reverse, says Gunn, of the usual situation in which participants are reluctant to talk. Most criminals and witnesses are "not happy" when it comes to being interviewed or interrogated—whereas Haines seemed to thrive on gabbing from the minute he was picked up in Lindsay.

In spite of Haines's overconfidence and willingness to talk to the police before the trial, Gunn insists there was no single moment or turn of events that decided the case. "There is no one thing in any trial" that turns the tide toward a conviction, he says. In other words, it's not like courtroom dramas on TV, where last-minute revelations shock the judge and jury.

He says that in evaluating a case, he asks two questions: are there reasonable grounds to obtain a conviction, and is the pursuit of a conviction in the public's best interests. At some point in the analysis of evidence, he arrives at a "threshold" where the answers to those questions become clear.

Gunn says Andy Copp and Cari Watson (Haines's ex-girlfriend) were the two most "probative" witnesses during the proceedings, meaning their testimony didn't consist of a mere single point or question. Gunn was able to explore their thinking, probing and drawing out their thoughts for absorption and consideration by the jury. Their styles—talkative and editorializing—allowed Gunn to draw out whatever they were thinking.

He says he wasn't overwhelmed by the media frenzy surrounding the case. There's a communications person in the prosecutions office, providing a buffer between the media and Gunn. At no time did he speak to the media about the matter. It was vital for Gunn to remain "mindful of my obligations and to conduct myself according to my obligations," he says.

In his day-to-day, out-of-the-courtroom social interactions, many of Gunn's friends peppered him with light queries and comments concerning the case. He made it his practice to simply "wink and move on," leaving curiosity-seekers to draw their own conclusions.

THE DEFENCE LAWYER

It almost seems like Ron "the Cat" Morris was handpicked by some higher power to be the defence lawyer for the Canadian Beer Bandit. For Morris, you see, is not your run-of-the-mill barrister.

The Cat, with his shock-white beard and hair, easily reddened complexion, and flashing blue eyes, is a wonderfully affable cross between a stout Kenny Rogers and the Kris Kringle character from the original *Miracle on 34th Street*. Morris works hard and plays hard. He enjoys his rum with water and ice. He came by the nick-name "Cat" honestly, having developed a reputation for speed and agility while playing goal for the St. F.X. hockey team in Antigonish and later, for the St. Thomas University Tommies.

He is also legendary for his revelry. One story has it that at Halifax's famous sports shrine, the Midtown Tavern, he took it upon himself to "teach" Billy Smith, the four-time Stanley Cup–winning goaltender for the New York Islanders, how to make a toe save. This demonstration reportedly involved acrobatic stretches and gyrations in the middle of the tavern floor. Only the Cat could get away such antics. Smith is obviously a good sport with a great sense of humour.

In the same vein, it has become a tradition on the Saturday be-fore each year's Golf Classic in Digby, Nova Scotia, for Morris and friends to spend a night in Halifax warming up for the party-hardy Digby event. Part of the tradition involves Morris leaving his Halifax hotel room on a risqué mid-afternoon jaunt to Bearly's Blues Bar and Grill. Nattily attired in flip flops and a Delta Barrington robe, the Cat would proceed to drink his trademark white rum from a bowl—cats only drink from bowls, after all. He is also famous for an exchange with one of Halifax's finer female bartenders at Cheers, which is part of the group of bars collectively known as the Liquor Dome. When asked if his preference would be "a single or a double," the Cat replied: "My dear, a double of course. I haven't had a single since I played peewee!"

Morris has been practising for twenty-five years; eighty-five to ninety percent of his caseload is criminal law, including the odd murder case. In short, he's no greenhorn. Nor was he new to the acquaintance of Wade Haines, whose case he ended up doing for free because he believed in his innocence. Morris is convinced that Haines got no money from the heist—not a penny, he insists.

Asked how he knew that Haines had no money to pay for his defence, beer-theft proceeds or no beer-theft proceeds, Morris replies: "I just knew." He says it with a wry grin, as though he'd done an underworld Dunn and Bradstreet check on his client. "You just know," he adds.

"I always had it in my mind that somebody else did this," says Morris, "that somebody got financial reward out of it, and I just knew Haines didn't. That's why I did the trial for nothing. And because that's how interesting I thought the case was."

"I knew Wade from being around Oromocto and I always liked the kid, actually," continues Morris, explaining why he took the case. "I had defended him since he was a kid, pretty much any time he got into trouble. He was always into areas involving fraud, like bad cheques. Just stuff. You know, you'd call it stupid stuff that he'd do for not very good reasons. None of it ever paid off."

The Beer Bandit case began during New Brunswick's legal-aid strike, which meant Morris couldn't take a legal-aid certificate to pay for his work. Doing so would have made Morris a scab labourer, which he wanted absolutely no part of. "I was on the legal aid list but we were still trying to keep solidarity. I'm not normally a duty counsellor, but my name was on the list. So I could've gotten paid through legal aid if I'd have taken the certificate, but because of the strike I wouldn't take the certificate. I was thinking to myself, 'Well, maybe this strike won't last, maybe there will be a certificate before the trial comes up.' But it just didn't happen that way and since I was so into the case, I figured I'm not going to jump ship on him now."

"Ron is a great guy," says Haines. "I think, though, that he was very busy. I wish I'd had money and a lawyer with more time. But I don't think Ron lost. We lost on the uncorroborated testimony of Andy Copp."

Cari Watson didn't help matters either, says Haines. He believes her testimony consisted of things that she had heard elsewhere, such as her claim that Haines was going to give her money he had obtained from the heist. It's from the testimony of those two individuals, Haines insists, that the trial turned against him and Morris.

Morris says Haines's case was an interesting one because the evidence was wholly circumstantial. "Whenever there's a circumstantial case, there's room to play with it. This case was certainly interesting. You know, I don't want to call it a fun case, because it wasn't. Most judge and jury trials are very arduous, very draining and very demanding. Even though as a lawyer you still had that drain on you, it was at least a case where nobody had been killed or slaughtered or anything like that. So at least in that respect, it was fun to do."

When Morris talks about the colourful witnesses, he describes them almost as though they'd been cast from an episode of *Trailer Park Boys* or *O Brother, Where Art Thou?* The jury laughed a lot, which has happened in other trials, he says, but not to the degree experienced during the Beer Bandit trial. "There were some real fun moments," he admits.

One moment that was not fun was the delivery of the verdict. Haines was declared guilty after just ninety minutes of deliberation, on February 11, 2005. Equally lacking in fun was the day of sentencing, when Justice Paulette Garnett sentenced Morris's client to nineteen and a half months in jail.

Throughout the trial, Morris felt they had a good jury, comprised of five women and seven men, who were drawn from a pool of three hundred possibilities. Morris says that the decision to go judge-and-jury instead of judge-only wasn't the primary reason for the guilty verdict. "One problem was that it was always in the forefront of the media attention. Moosehead kept it up and they actually, in the end, they benefited out of it. But it always kept coming up in the media." Morris says the media almost seemed to presume Haines's guilt. He insists that this continuous media attention certainly had an effect on the outcome of the trial.

"With a jury, you don't know for sure how much they've read or heard," he explains. "When I first went into it, I didn't think that the early publicity would have affected it, but I think now that it really did. Haines kept saying that to me. He kept saying, like, 'Jeez, how could I not be found guilty. They had me guilty from the first day that they went up to Ontario to get me.'"

Having said that, Morris acknowledges that during the trial itself, the media were fair. "Any statements I made, I thought they presented them the way it was intended. As a matter of fact, I was using the media a bit to reinforce the fact that the case was circumstantial." Morris says the media played the case that way right up until the end—until Cari Watson testified.

He adds that a Canadian defence lawyer's scrutiny of potential jurors is not like the American system that most of us know from movies and TV shows. Lawyers in Canada don't normally ask detailed questions of potential jurors; they go on basic information, such as who the person is, their age, occupation, gender, and so on. "There are provisions that if you thought there was prejudice, you could set it up and ask questions," explains Morris, "but in these types of cases it's rare."

The four key things that baked Haines, according to Morris, were the relentless media exposure, the testimony of Cari Watson, the hilarious testimony of Andy Copp, and Haines's statement to the RCMP when they originally hooked up in Lindsay.

"The statement was very foolish," says Morris. "I said to him, 'If you had called me before they got hold of you in Ontario, if you had shut your mouth, you'd have never even been charged.' They never would have charged him if he hadn't told them this ridiculous story." One critical aspect of Haines's story was that he'd hitchhiked from Fredericton and been picked up by a man from Quebec driving a black Ford F-150 half-ton truck. They hadn't spoken much on the journey through to Rivière-du-Loup, Quebec, where the man with limited English was supposedly destined. Haines has always maintained that they had made one stop along the way.

"Wade couldn't supply the driver's name or anything," says Morris, "but he told me that they stopped in Woodstock at the new Esso place, so I actually went and searched there because I was doing trials in Woodstock anyway. I went there to see if they had video surveillance or anything like that to see if we could get a licence number on this truck. Because if we could have found this supposed guy that drove him between Fredericton and Rivière-du-Loup…well. But we couldn't find him. There was no video unit at the gas station, which, it being new, I was surprised about."

Morris even considered putting ads in the Rivière-du-Loup newspapers asking the driver to come forward. He feels that the trial might have had a different outcome if he had found the guy, and if Haines had kept his mouth shut when he went in for police questioning. "They'd have had nothing if he'd said nothing," Morris insists. "What could they do or say? They had him picking up the beer on the Friday and that's all they had."

Morris admits that even with Haines's "foolish story," there was the possibility he could have gotten through the trial without being convicted. "We had evidence in the trial that he had done something like this before." In that previous incident, Haines had kept the truck, and the trucking company had had to come with the police to retrieve it—with the load still on it. When Cari Watson took the stand, Morris's trial plan of action really started to fall apart, he claims.

"The girlfriend turned on him," says Morris. "She made some statements about what he had said to her that really cooked him. It had to do with his saying something about where the truck was parked in Grand Falls, and he supposedly said to her, 'It was supposed to look that way.' And she said that he wanted to know her bank account number because someone was going to deposit $2,000 into it. There were five or six little things that nailed the top on it. She was a very telling witness."

What made Watson's testimony that much worse for Morris and his client was what Morris sees as a lack of disclosure on the part of the police. "Usually when you're doing a case you have all the evidence months beforehand, but in this particular case, the evidence kept coming in piecemeal. They were even disclosing new stuff to us just a couple of days before the trial," he says.

"I actually thought they [the RCMP and the prosecution] were thinking that it wasn't going to trial, that there might have been a plea on it or something," Morris continues. "We didn't know anything about what the girlfriend was going to say until right at the thirteenth hour. They're supposed to disclose everything they've got, but in this case, the investigator went back out to ask her about something. He [Pierre Gervais] is such a likeable guy and so smooth—I used to say to him when he was doing under-cover work, 'You look more like a criminal than the criminals.' He got out there (at her house) chatting with her and suddenly he got a whole new statement out of her, right about the time of the trial, about the truck in Grand Falls, about the $2,000.

"We weren't anticipating her being onto that. She didn't say anything about this stuff at the show of cause, and she said he [Haines] told her about this stuff after the show of cause, which could have been true. He couldn't keep his mouth shut. If only he'd have kept his mouth shut. He screwed himself eight ways to Sunday. I think he really felt that that story of his was going to fly."

The other damning testimony came from the inimitable Andy Copp. According to Morris, Copp was so honest about his cocaine habits and some related stories that he was very believable. "In the end, they [the jury] said, 'Well, he told everything else, why wouldn't he tell the truth about [Haines].'"

Morris and others agree that Copp took the trial to a level of hilarity rarely seen in New Brunswick courtrooms. "I've never seen anybody that funny on the witness stand," says Morris, whose facial and vocal imitations of Copp are priceless in their own right.

Copp had been in a serious car accident years earlier, which cost him his right leg but earned him $250,000 in insurance compensation. Under cross-examination, Morris said, "Now, Mr. Copp, you've got a bad cocaine habit."

"And this is the way he answered me," recalls Morris. "He says, 'Uh-huh, I guess maybe I do.' Everything was just that way. I said, 'Well, you got a big settlement when you lost your leg in an auto accident?' And Copp replied something to the effect, 'Yup, $250,000 I got,' and I said, 'That's a fair amount of money. What did you do with it?'"

Copp reacted with a matter-of-fact response that sent the courtroom reeling: "I bought a pair of sneakers, a '94 Firebird, and the rest went to cocaine."

"Just like that," says Morris, "and the jury just gets pissing themselves laughing. He was supposedly hooked up with the Hell's Angels out of Grand Falls at one time. But he was awful funny."

In spite of a series of official admonitions from the bench, at some point in time—perhaps over cocktails with her peers, or in a future discussion with her grandchildren, or perhaps in her memoirs—Justice Paulette Garnett will have to reminisce fondly about the lighter moments of the Beer Bandit trial. As criminal events go, this was a memorable gem of a trial, a gift like few others. People don't remember the late American lawyer Johnnie Cochrane, after all, for his civil or divorce work; it was all about the theatrics of the O. J. Simpson trial and the gloves that didn't fit.

But behind that poker face, if Justice Garnett did find aspects of the trial humorous, she sure as hell wasn't letting on. "At least some members of the press have treated this crime as if it was a joke," Garnett was quoted as remarking to the court, as she sentenced Haines. "Why stealing beer is any funnier than stealing anything else is beyond me. It's a serious crime."

The judge said she was not amused by the international attention given to the trial. Nor was she moved by Ron Morris's attempt to argue that Moosehead actually benefited from the crime. "I don't care how much free publicity they got," she said. "They still had beer stolen."

As the individual responsible for Haines's proper representation, Morris confesses to having some regrets about the decision to go with a jury trial, especially because of what happened when Justice Garnett charged the jury before retiring them to deliberate.

Morris explains: "Unless I read her totally wrong, the way her charge came out, I felt it was in our favour and I took from that, that if she had been rendering a decision, she might have acquitted. I could be reading her totally wrong. I remember saying to Wade, 'You know, Wade,' and I looked at him and said, 'I think we made the wrong election,' and he said, 'Yeah, we might have.' It was on my advice to some extent."

Morris says he simply thought that a jury would not buy into a circumstantial case, whereas a judge might. Typically that's true, but he says it's almost impossible to predict what will happen in these situations.

Haines has one major regret: the decision not to pursue an appeal. If they had appealed, it's possible he might have been brought to testify, which he didn't do at trial. Asked why he didn't appeal, he says he did not want to hurt his mother any more than he already had. The relentless media exposure of the heist, the trial, and all the rest was enough.

PART IV

BECOMING THE BEER BANDIT

THE TRIAL

The Beer Bandit appeared before Justice Paulette Garnett of the Court of Queen's Bench for jury selection and the beginning of his trial on Tuesday, February 8, 2005. Prosecutors Cameron Gunn and Trent Wilson lined up their circumstantial evidence, beginning with a single six-pack of the distinctive Spanish-labelled lager. Haines was represented by Ron "the Cat" Morris and his assistant, Elan MacPhee.

The case hinged on the basic fact that Haines was supposed to be driving the truck at the time the beer was stolen.

The Canadian Press account of the proceedings was carried across the nation:

> "We're not asserting Wade Haines acted alone," Crown prosecutor Wilson said as he made his opening remarks to the jury. "Common sense tells us he could not have acted alone, but we intend to prove that he was involved."

The case appeared simple enough. Haines was the driver. The truck was found on August 17 in a mall parking lot in Grand Falls, New Brunswick, with the engine still running and Haines nowhere in sight. The beer, $70,000 worth of suds, was gone.

Don MacPherson wrote accounts of Trent Wilson's courtroom presentation in the Fredericton *Daily Gleaner*:

> *"This is going to be about common sense," Crown Prosecutor Trent Wilson told the jurors Tuesday in an opening statement. "The evidence for the Crown in this case is circumstantial."*

The lack of eyewitnesses did not discourage the prosecuting attorneys. Wilson is reported to have used the time-worn analogy that if one went to sleep at night having seen that the lawn was green, and then awoke the next morning to a thick blanket of white, one could reasonably assume that it had snowed overnight, even if one hadn't witnessed the snowfall itself. "There's really no mystery to it," said Wilson, backed by his snow story.

The trial lasted a total of four days, presenting witnesses as disparate as Haines's ex-girlfriend Cari Watson, the prosthetic witness Andy Copp, and two Moosehead employees, Angela Gilbert and Barry Green.

Gilbert and Green testified that they'd met Haines at the Moosehead Breweries shipping area on Friday, August 13, when he picked up the load of Mexico-destined beer. MacPherson reported in the *Gleaner* that "both said Haines was behaving normally and nothing seemed amiss." The two also testified about the shipment paperwork Haines would have had with him in the truck, including information that identified what was in the shipment, the trailer number, and the licence plate number of the trailer. Gilbert and Green responded to defence questioning by editorializing about the potential benefits accruing to Moosehead from free publicity, and by speculating about how long it would take to unload a tractor-trailer full of beer by hand.

Brenway Transport employee Jeff Barry testified that Haines had picked up the trailer from the company yard in Fredericton on the afternoon of Friday, August 13, before heading to the Moosehead plant in Saint John and then returning with the trailer full of beer. Barry said that when he stopped by the office on Sunday evening, he noticed that the trailer was still in the yard.

Don MacPherson wrote of Barry's testimony:

"Most of the drivers tend to leave later. They want to spend a little more time at home."

The trailer was gone by Monday morning, but it never arrived in Ontario, Barry said. Brenway staff couldn't reach Haines and the truck's tracking system wasn't sending out a signal and the satellite system had stopped reporting the night of August 15.

Barry said the police were called Tuesday, and the truck and the trailer were located in the parking lot of a Grand Falls mall, empty of all but a few cases of the Mexican market beer.

He said he and the company owner went to Grand Falls to retrieve the truck after police personnel were finished processing it.

Upon arriving back in Fredericton, Barry said, it was discovered that the satellite tracking system had been deliberately disconnected.

A knife was also found in the trailer itself, lodged in a metal brace, Barry said. He didn't know how police investigators missed finding it.

Barry also testified it was the company that finally determined where Haines was. He said Haines used a Brenway calling card August 23 to place calls from Lindsay, Ontario, to various numbers in Fredericton and Doaktown.

The transport company had kept the calling card active in case Haines decided to use it, Barry said, and Aliant notified him when it was used.

Under cross-examination by Ron "the Cat" Morris, Barry said that a security guard is posted at the Brenway yard throughout the night, but if a truck came in and hauled away a trailer, the guard likely wouldn't give it a second look.

This might prompt readers to wonder if a company such as Brenway, responsible for hauling shipments worth many thousands of dollars, couldn't require such a security guard to oversee the signing out or formal release of a trailer by authorized personnel. One might also wonder: what does the security guard do?

On the third day of the trial, February 10, 2005, a videotape of Haines's initial interview with the RCMP was played before the jury. The written statement that Haines had given to Cpl. Jackson and Cst. Gervais was also read into the record. Haines, however, did not testify. In both the videotape and the written statement, Haines maintained he had nothing to do with the theft.

MacPherson reported in the *Gleaner* that after the dressing-down from the Brenway mechanic (for parking the truck on an incline and draining the fuel from one tank to the next), Haines was upset enough to change his mind about delivering the beer shipment to Ontario.

"When I awoke on Sunday, August 15, I decided to pack my stuff and go to Ontario," he wrote in his written statement.
He said he left the truck unlocked with the keys in the ignition.
"I jumped on the highway and hitchhiked to Rivière-du-Loup," he said on the videotape.

He eventually took a bus from there to visit his aunt in Lindsay, Ontario, he said.

Haines told police he had received a replacement paycheque from his employer a few days before and ended up cashing it and the original cheque after he'd found it.

He said he knew he was going to lose his job, and that combined with a bad argument with his girlfriend and a pending court appearance on another matter, made him decide to get away from his problems for a while.

In later testimony that same day, Cpl. Kevin Jackson was reported to have said that there were a number of things about Haines's story that just didn't make sense.

"The story, in my opinion, was highly improbable," he said.

He wondered why Haines didn't contact the police, his girlfriend, his employer, or his mother after he read [in the Toronto *Sun*] *that he had been reported missing.*

On cross-examination by Ron Morris, Jackson admitted that he was surprised Haines hadn't fled after he learned RCMP investigators were coming to Ontario to question him. According to MacPherson's account,

He said it was the first time under such circumstances that a suspect hadn't fled on him.

Jackson said he believes Haines didn't flee because he was over-confident. He said Haines is an intelligent guy who believed he'd concocted a scenario that would leave him in the clear.

"He had his story prepared and rehearsed in his mind,"
Jackson said.

Another RCMP official, Cpl. Paul Gagnon, a forensic identification specialist, testified that he had examined the truck and found no fingerprints belonging to Haines, but that he did find prints belonging to two men identified as Haines's friends: Darren Kelly and Wayne Dutcher. Gagnon said he could identify the prints of Kelly and Dutcher because both had criminal histories.

The afternoon of February 9 was the most revealing and colourful moment of the entire trial. The focus was Victor Andrew Copp of Plaster Rock. The following is Don MacPherson's version of the proceedings:

> *Copp* [in responding to Crown questioning] *said one day last summer—he couldn't remember the exact date—Haines had approached him and asked him where he could sell a load of beer.*
>
> *"Do you know where I could get rid of a load? Do you know what a load of beer is worth?" Copp quoted Haines as saying.*
>
> [Copp] *said he and Haines had been hanging out with mutual friends, but that exchange occurred when the two of them were alone.*
>
> *When Crown prosecutor Trent Wilson asked Copp why Haines would think he'd know how to dispose of stolen beer, Copp said there were a number of reasons.*
>
> *He said he used to have some connections with the Hell's Angels.*
>
> *"I knew some bikers years ago, and they'll do anything," he said.*
>
> *Copp said he looks like the type of guy who knows how criminal activity works.*

He said the brief exchange with Haines occurred at the Millville home of Vince Sharpe.

Copp said they had gone there because Sharpe owed him money.

After Haines had approached him, Copp said, he spoke with Sharpe.

Sharpe then spoke with Copp and said Haines had asked him about unloading stolen beer as well.

Copp said he told Sharpe to steer clear of the situation.

He said Sharpe paid him some of the money he owed for a pickup truck and had given him some cocaine.

Copp went on during the trail to talk about his accident, the insurance money, his addiction to cocaine and his lack of esteem for Haines:

"He's not my favourite cup of tea, no," he told [Ron] Morris under cross-examination. "I don't like some of the choices he's made. I don't hate the man."

He said he would never lie in order to send someone to jail.

He did admit that as recently as the day before, he might have told someone, "I don't care if he rots in jail."

Earlier in his testimony, Copp is reported to have said that although he had nothing to do with the heist, he did find twenty-five to thirty cases of the stolen beer in the woods in Penniac, where he liked to go to get high. He said he had planned to sell the beer, but it was gone when he came back to retrieve it. Copp also admitted he was hired to deliver the stolen beer for someone but never got paid.

Copp's dislike of Haines is apparently reciprocated; when I interviewed Haines at the Saint John Regional Correctional Centre, he did not express any love for Copp. At the jail, Haines had hooked up with another inmate, who had a few things to say about Copp. The inmate is a self-confessed drug dealer who, it was agreed during a telephone call, will remain nameless. Given that Copp was so ready and willing to tell the trial division court about his cocaine habit, little of what follows is speaking out of school.

After Copp's quarter-million-dollar cocaine spending spree, his access to pocket change, unbelievably, became scarce. So, according to the anonymous jail source, Copp developed the habit of hocking his prosthetic leg in order to obtain cash loans for his drug of choice. For extended periods, Copp would go about "tripping" on his one good leg; whenever he would come into some money, he would turn around and redeem the prosthetic leg. It was, after all, better than your average TV or watch: it's a twenty-thousand-dollar piece of equipment.

And Haines's jailed dealer buddy had more to say. He said he knew fellas who knew fellas who knew fellas who had first hand knowledge about twelve hundred cans of the stolen Moosehead. They had the brilliantly simple idea of hiding the stash in culverts in the Penniac area, outside Fredericton. Culverts are, of course, way off the beaten track—they're generally the province of little boys hunting frogs or fulfilling dares. The RCMP, like most people, have an aversion to rooting around in culverts. In addition to being an ideal hiding place, culverts are also dark and cold. Beer, of course, tastes better cold. So, somewhere in a culvert near Penniac, twelve hundred cans of Moosehead remain perfectly chilled and ready for consumption on a hot summer's day.

As a February storm raged outside, the final day of the trial focused on the testimony of Haines's ex-girlfriend, Cari Watson. She talked about her now-infamous birthday cards signed by the "Beer Bandit," saying she thought it was all a joke and laughed about the inscription when she received and read them.

Watson admitted under examination from Crown prosecutor Gunn that she'd been a long-time cocaine user and addict, having first used drugs when she was just thirteen years old and continuing to do so until she was twenty-three. Like everyone else, she said she'd been clean for about a year. Watson also admitted that she had failed to report income—money she'd received from Haines—while on social assistance from the Province of New Brunswick.

Under cross-examination from assistant defence counsel Elan MacPhee, Watson admitted that she had once joked to Haines about stealing a shipment of booze. According to MacPherson, the *Gleaner* reporter, Watson was the one who raised the idea, and Haines did not react well to the suggestion:

> She knew Haines was scheduled to haul a load of beer August 15, but she didn't think she had mentioned it to anyone. She said she couldn't remember for certain.
> "I don't think so. I didn't really care," she said.

MacPherson wrote that Watson cried often during her testimony and got choked up. Justice Garnett called a recess at one point so Watson could gather herself.

"I'm not up here to hurt him. I still love him. I don't want him to hate me," Watson said in her testimony.

She said she was supposed to accompany Haines and the beer on the trip to Toronto, but he never picked her up. By most accounts, that kind of event was the norm in their on-again, off-again relationship.

Equally revealing of the unusual nature of their relationship is the fact that Cari Watson got a birthday card from Wade Haines—actually, two birthday cards from Wade Haines—even though she'd told him that she was pregnant with another man's baby, and even though she would testify against him a month later.

Since Haines had been in jail for months already, the cards he put together for Watson were handmade on plain folded-over white bond. On the front of each he wrote "Happy 24th", on the inside he inscribed a little poem, and on the back he wrote "Copyright 'Beer Bandit.'" The cards, says Haines, were intended for Watson's twenty-fourth birthday, on January 8, 2005.

It was her recollection of these cards that caught the attention of the Mounties, the prosecution, the media, and, obviously, the jury. From a distance, it could appear as though Haines was flaunting his crime, making light of it, taking too cavalier an attitude about his predicament. But having heard him describe first-hand how the invention of the cards came about, it seems more plausible to me that he created them on a lark and just for fun. Sitting idly in the Saint John Regional Correctional Centre, he had nothing else to do. It's easy to understand how, sitting in the lonely confines of such an institution, one's judgment can go more than just slightly askew—not as askew as on cocaine, perhaps, but askew nonetheless.

Haines says he didn't even invent the tag he's ended up wearing, although it seems there's still something he enjoys about it. During one interview, he even made a side inquiry about copyright and whether or not mailing something to one's self constitutes a form of copyright protection. If anyone holds the copyright to the phrase "Beer Bandit," it is an inmate at the Saint John Regional Correctional Centre, who remains unknown but who first came up with the nickname. The inmate had clipped a newspaper image of Haines and stuck it in the window of his cell door. The image carried the caption "Beer Bandit." So for months, Haines was taunted in jail about this nickname. The image was ever-present. After six months of seeing and hearing it repeatedly, signing Watson's birthday card with that name didn't seem like such a big deal to him. That is, at least, until it was entered into testimony.

The closing testimony heard the accounts of several witnesses who testified for the Crown about finding some of the stolen beer in ditches, along trails, and in the woods around Millville, Nackawic, East Newbridge, and Maple Ridge. As MacPherson wrote in the February 11 *Daily Gleaner,*

> *Previous testimony suggested Haines was in that area the day before the beer theft and had approached a couple of people—including Vincent Sharpe of Maple Ridge—about how he could unload some stolen beer.*
>
> *District 2 RCMP Cst. Cara Paul testified she found an abandoned Chevy Cavalier on October 2. The windows were down, the radio was missing and there was a screwdriver on the driver's seat.*
>
> *There was also a can of Spanish-labelled Moosehead beer under a seat, Paul said. She reported the finding to investigators and discovered the vehicle was registered to Sharpe.*
>
> *Sharpe has not been charged in connection with the beer heist case.*

Victim impact statements have become increasingly common in North American courtrooms. We normally think of them as having to do with personal loss or torment, but corporations, as legal "persons," can be victims, too. In that capacity, Moosehead Breweries Ltd. submitted the following statement to the court near the conclusion of Haines's trial:

> *The impact of this theft should be separated into three catego-*
> *ries. First of all, the theft of the beer did not result in a direct*
> *monetary loss because Moosehead has filed an insurance claim*
> *with its carrier. Presumably we will recover the actual cost of*
> *the goods at some future time.*
>
> *However, it is the intangible effects of the crime that had a*
> *greater impact on our business. The 4,200 cases of stolen beer*
> *were being shipped to an important foreign customer. This*
> *large Mexican retailer was entering its busiest beer-selling*
> *season and Moosehead Breweries was working overtime to*
> *fill the customer's orders. The loss of the shipment could not*
> *have come at a worse time for us and our customer. The beer*
> *business is very competitive and a lost sale is never made up.*
> *In other words, a case of beer not sold today for any reason is*
> *permanently lost, either because the consumer has decided not*
> *to drink beer today, or because the consumer has purchased*
> *a different brand. So, when a beer retailer is out of stock of*
> *Moosehead and a Moosehead consumer wants a case of beer,*
> *he or she will purchase another brand. The sale is lost forever*
> *and, perhaps worst of all, the consumer may permanently*
> *switch his or her preference to the competing brand. To put this*
> *in perspective relative to the beer theft, 4,200 consumers were*
> *unable to buy a case of Moosehead beer because the product*

did not reach its destination. This was not only bad news for Moosehead, but also for the retailer in Mexico.

The third issue relates to the amount of work the theft created for employees of Moosehead. The department most impacted by the theft was our traffic [i.e. shipping] department. The theft resulted in hundreds of hours of additional work for those employees. The work included our fruitless attempts to find the shipment before the theft was discovered, the disruption of work to assist with the police investigation, the cost and effort in having numerous "finds" of recovered beer retrieved and destroyed, and the work involved in dealing with our Mexican customer on the issue of the stolen product. Unfortunately, the stolen beer could not be replaced with a new order because beer takes approximately 30 days to brew and package.

Finally, it is our sincere hope that the Court will address the issue of truck hijacking when considering the sentence for Mr. Haines. This is a very serious issue for shippers and carriers. The safety and security of truck drivers, of the goods they transport, and of the public in general, must be considered. We believe a message must be sent to the criminal element that the Courts will not tolerate thefts of this nature.

The trial, as we know, ended when the jury took only ninety minutes to find Haines guilty, sending him into the custody of the Saint John Regional Correctional Centre and, ultimately, the Westmoreland Minimum Security Institution in Dorchester.

THE MEDIA

Everyone admits that an integral part of the public's fascination with the Beer Bandit caper is the fact that the beer was destined for Mexico. It was the perfect additional twist for an already bent and twisted story. Canadians, by and large, understand as much about Mexico and the Mexican people as Americans do about Canada and the Canadian people—in other words, not much. The Mexican angle, informed by our pop-culture stereotypes—Clint Eastwood arriving by horseback in a dusty Mexican town, Brad Pitt comically caught in a saloon when a Mexican drug deal goes awry, siestas, Speedy Gonzales, the Frito Bandito—was decisive in piquing the public's interest. It also didn't hurt that the stuff that got stolen was beer—and one of Canada's best loved beers at that.

If the cargo in that missing trailer had been a shipment of Sealy mattresses or Majesta paper towels or fifty thousand cartons of orange juice, destined simply for Toronto or New York, the story would have evaporated after a short burst of newscasts. "Beer Bandit" would not be in our vocabulary and Wade Haines might never even have been charged, let alone convicted. It was the combination of Mexico, Moosehead, and Mounties that cast our eyes due Haines-ward.

Moncton *Times and Transcript* staff writer Rod Allen perfectly captured what was undoubtedly the attitude of many members of the media. Writing retrospectively in the January 1, 2005, edition of the paper about the "real whodrunkit," he argued that "however secretly and guiltily," reporters and headline writers were "grateful in the doldrums of the summer 'silly' season" for the Beer Bandit story. As mentioned earlier, reporters and editors are known to languish in the normally dry news days of summer, as though news takes a hiatus, like Quebec construction workers during their annual two-week shutdown.

Although he had a hand in it, Wade Haines wasn't the one who gave the Beer Bandit story its everlasting life. And although Moosehead and its PR guys helped prolong the story, they were just catalysts. In the end, it wasn't really even the media that drove the story. It was the public. The general public seemed to crave the entertainment of this odd-ball of a story, and even seemed prepared to make Haines into a minor cult figure or folk hero.

Julie Caswell, a veteran Halifax-based ATV News producer, recalls that she and her associates tracked the story vigorously when it broke, giving it successive days of profile near the top of their newscasts because they instinctively knew "it was the story everybody was talking about." She says they discussed the story's merits as it unfolded day by day, and "categorized" it as a story that had a prominent place in the public's mind.

"It was unusual," she says. "It had all of the elements" of a story that is sure to stick: the oddity of fifty thousand cans of beer being stolen, the Mexican connection, and the fact that Haines had gone missing, which added to the initial intrigue.

Caswell says it was the kind of story that people are absolutely certain to remember. It wasn't "going to change people's lives," but like other fascinating yarns about everyday people, "it had that ring to it," the ring that a seasoned news professional knows the public wants to hear.

It didn't hurt matters, she says, that "Moosehead cooperated quite a bit" in helping get the story to air—as evidenced by Joel Levesque's quick and ready provision of video footage of the brewery and its workings.

Caswell recalls a fun piece done by ATV's Fredericton-based journalist Andy Campbell, which focused on the public's interaction with both the story and the crime. Campbell began the coverage with this intro: "It sounds like a truly Canadian pastime—hunting for beer." The idea that New Brunswickers were out and about searching for the missing Moosehead wasn't wholly fabricated, either: individuals were coming forward with single cans of beer, and there were the incidents involving the discovery of a marijuana grow op near Blackville and the errant trailer full of beer that landed in Owen Lawson's pasture in East Newbridge.

Don MacPherson is a crime-beat reporter in a region where you can count crime-beat reporters on your fingers. He's one of those low-key, unassuming guys whose wit sneaks up on you. He's got a sleeper of a personality, with ideas, thoughts and comments that go deeper than you'd expect, that are acerbic and can sting and make you laugh. He's very slyly aware, you might say, which is a useful quality for a crime-beat journalist.

Since joining the newsroom of the Fredericton *Daily Gleaner* in 2001, MacPherson has covered the full range of criminal matters— robbery, murder, rape, and everything else. He took his English degree from St. Francis Xavier University in Antigonish, Nova Scotia, and topped it off with the year-long journalism program at Charlottetown's Holland College. When I met him at Fredericton's Lunar Rogue Pub, he waxed philosophical about Wade Haines and related events. There was a Moosehead Breweries product at the ready. "I'm an Alpine guy," he admits.

MacPherson says that without a doubt it was "absolutely" one of the most entertaining stories he's ever encountered in his decade-long career as a reporter. No other story seemed to have as much of a "multi-community" backdrop in New Brunswick. Every community has its case that emerges in the New Brunswick court system, says MacPherson, but the Beer Bandit caper seemed to have something for the widest possible variety of communities: Fredericton,

Woodstock, Penniac, Doaktown, Blackville, East Newbridge, Grand Falls (all in New Brunswick); Rivière-du-Loup, in Quebec; and Ottawa and Lindsay, in Ontario. It was spread out.

I interviewed MacPherson four months after the trial, so he'd had time to process the whole Beer Bandit phenomenon. Interestingly, he couldn't resist comparing it to various TV shows. It was "the Seinfeld story of the day," he says—a simple premise turned into a prolonged absurdity. "But for every funny story," he adds, "there's someone in pain."

Like many others, he likens the Beer Bandit story to an episode of *Trailer Park Boys*. The comparison is apt, he says, because all levels of the legal community are into the *Trailer Park Boys*. "There's more truth to it than fiction," says MacPherson. Spend an afternoon strolling around an Atlantic Canadian criminal courtroom and you get an immediate sense of what he means. The antics of Ricky, Bubbles, and company can be matched—personality to personality—to people in peril passing through the turnstiles of the New Brunswick legal system on any given day.

MacPherson is an astute television analyst. He sees Haines as "an *NYPD Blue* type of suspect," the kind you see in the precinct shooting his mouth off until he ends up convicting himself, revealing things he shouldn't reveal, trying to outsmart street-savvy cops who aren't about to be outsmarted or out-savvyed. MacPherson says the *NYPD Blue* suspect is the guy who, like Haines, just can't keep things to himself. The term "loose cannon" comes to mind. Conversely, the *Law and Order* suspect, whom MacPherson contrasts with Haines, is subdued, creative, and crafty. He makes the cops come to him, squeezing every little ounce of info out of him, giving almost nothing in return. Of course in *Law and Order*, the case always goes to trial, unlike in the real world. There's always an astonishing plot twist unearthed by criminological masterminds, and there's the subsequent closing revelation that alters the outcome of events. Haines, on the other hand, was sunk the day he was interviewed and interrogated in Lindsay.

The Beer Bandit charges and trial were another contribution to what MacPherson calls his "very own *Jerry Springer Show* that happens every single day." Haines, his coke-head associates and his troubled girlfriend made for a typical *Jerry Springer* cast. MacPherson calls Cari Watson "a very *Jerry Springer* girl."

The Beer Bandit caper was the one story that every single New Brunswicker cottoned onto, says MacPherson, with the possible exception of teetotallers. "It was every bit a New Brunswick story," he says.

Because MacPherson is in court basically all the time, he's become pretty adept at sizing up accused parties, their acts, and the people and events surrounding them—much like a judge. He calls Haines an "average blue-collar guy" who just happened to get into a lot of trouble. "He's just a ball-cap kind of guy," says MacPherson. Haines reminds him of a lot of guys who move through the justice system, kids from fairly decent households who appear to be on the right track, until the drugs creep in, they make the "tiniest mistake," and things seem to unravel. MacPherson sees Haines as a "fairly friendly guy" who didn't overreact even when the RCMP became increasingly accusatory in the courtroom. He never displayed any animosity toward the police.

Haines has been in court so many times, and has been involved in the non-violent criminal culture of Fredericton for so long, that sitting in court "was like reporting for work," notes MacPherson. For people like Haines, he says, "part of their job is going to court. It's his regular thing that he does. They are who they are. They have criminal records."

MacPherson spends a lot of time focusing on and analyzing whoever's testifying during trials. Of Cari Watson, he says she chose her words on the stand very carefully, as though she was trying very hard not to incriminate either herself or Haines. "She was very unhappy to be there," MacPherson says. She was hostile to both the defence and the prosecution, even though she was a prosecution witness. "She was all over the map emotionally."

MacPherson says Andy Copp, the former cocaine addict with the prosthetic leg, "was an interesting witness because you could tell he was holding back." He found Copp interesting to watch in court because when people have a serious history with drugs, "no one knows what they're going to say in the witness stand"—not the police, not the prosecution, not the defence.

He describes Copp as a guy with long, curly hair, a guy who looked unkempt, as he limped to the stand. Copp testified that he'd been clean for several months preceding the trial and his testimony, but MacPherson has a theory about that. "It's funny how all these types of witnesses all just recently gave up drugs, how they're all-of-a-sudden clean." These oft-repeated claims sound a little too convenient for MacPherson.

But no matter what Copp or Watson had to say, MacPherson is convinced it was the accused's own statements to police that did him in. Of the hypothesis that someone Haines had been doing drugs with that weekend jumped into the tractor-trailer parked on the fringe of Fredericton, drove to the Brenway yard, and hauled the beer to Grand Falls, MacPherson is more than skeptical. "How many people can drive a big truck like that? Those things are not easy to move. It's not like jumping into a Cavalier and just driving off."

"I think Haines himself swung it," MacPherson insists. "The jury needed an explanation. The defence planted seeds but they didn't water that plant. The fact [that] his story didn't make sense created a sense of deception."

MacPherson does believe Haines's statement that he made no profit from the venture. He says no one could have profited because no one wanted to have the easily identifiable hot goods in their possession. Having just one can of the stuff would be tanta-mount to a public proclamation of guilt. He suspects that the plan was to sell large quantities of the beer to various bootleggers, and that the Penniac area probably would have been a prime outlet for distribution. The connection to drugs would have been there.

"If you spend any amount of time in court at all, you constantly hear about Penniac," says MacPherson.

Of all the witnesses, MacPherson seems to have a soft spot for farmer Owen Lawson, whom he describes as "just a hard-working guy who never before caught a whiff of anything like this. He's just an honest, hard-working guy."

MacPherson says he was intrigued by the makeup of the legal teams in the trial, pointing out that two relatively junior mem-bers of the Fredericton legal community played significant roles in the courtroom. The more senior and experienced crown pros-ecutor Cameron Gunn, he says, provided a "grooming" oppor-tunity for assistant counsel Trent Wilson. And it was unusual for the defence to have a backup since it wasn't a murder trial. Ron Morris's assistant in the case, up-and-coming Fredericton lawyer Elan MacPhee, also conducted a fair bit of examination. She was especially useful for the defence team, MacPherson believes, be-cause it's good to have a female lawyer for the softer handling of female witnesses, especially one who was as potentially hostile as Cari Watson.

MacPherson is skeptical of Moosehead's claims of victimization. He says he wouldn't be the least bit surprised if the brewery de-cided to release six-packs of Spanish-labelled Moosehead Lager in the Maritimes, as a publicity stunt. "Everybody in New Brunswick will buy a six-pack," he predicts. "Two-four buyers will come into the liquor store that day and buy eighteen of what they usually drink [if it's not already Moosehead] and then pick up a six-pack of the Spanish-labelled beer for themselves," or for ex-pat relatives elsewhere in the country. The only thing that might deter the company, he believes, would be the legal issues involved with putting product that looks like evidence into the open marketplace.

Frank Matys had as much fun with Haines's ordeal as any other writer. A columnist in *Orillia Today*—coincidentally the home turf of the late, great humourist Stephen Leacock, who would have thrived on the Beer Bandit caper—Matys wrote shortly after Haines's February 11 conviction that beer drinkers "everywhere" would rejoice at the news of the jury's findings.

> *In order to fully appreciate the gravity of this heinous crime,*
> *it is necessary to put the above-mentioned figure* [referring
> to the volume of stolen product] *in perspective: 50,000 cans*
> *of beer would fill six Olympic-size swimming pools, or feed a*
> *dozen underprivileged bar flies for the better part of a month.*
> *(In truth, I have no idea whether 50,000 cans of beer would fill*
> *six Olympic-size pools, but the image of someone swimming*
> *laps in a small lake of lager is certainly stunning).*

Matys went on to say that those who rely on beer to "slake our thirst during the humid summer months" would be holding solemn memorials outside Ontario beer stores, "a genuinely heartfelt action that garners some strange looks from our wives."

Of course the beer was not destined for Orillia, or anywhere in Ontario for that matter, but because Matys is a columnist, he can editorialize, exaggerate, and apply his wit in whatever way makes for the most entertaining reading. He even managed to find an Ontario angle for the Beer Bandit heist:

*It is safe to say this is the one and only time beer drinkers have
taken an interest in anything that happens inside Canada's
court system, unless of course you count the marijuana grow
operation uncovered at Barrie's former Molson plant.*

Matys was referring to what police in Ontario say was "the largest and most sophisticated grow operation in Canada," the discovery in Barrie on January 17, 2004, of more than 30,000 marijuana
plants in an old Molson brewing plant that had been abandoned
four years earlier. Scores of officers and K-9 teams descended upon
the site, resulting in the arrests of nine people from St. Catherines,
the Niagara region, and Toronto. The force found 60,000 square
feet of space, housing all the ingredients necessary for a major drug
operation. The site could house up to fifty people in a dormitory
style arrangements of beds. There were televisions, refrigerators,
stoves, and all the hydroponic growing gizmos needed to feed and
fuel an indoor marijuana "farm."

"As you can well imagine," wrote Matys, "beer drinkers were
very disappointed to learn there wasn't any actual beer involved
in the brewery bust. Just acres and acres of illegal pot that, unlike
beer, tastes quite lousy, no matter how long you refrigerate it."

Ron Barry, op-ed page editor of the Saint John *Telegraph-Journal*,
took on the system in a piece he wrote after Haines's conviction,
concluding that the others who must have aided in the heist should
be brought to justice.

*The Moosehead theft provoked a lot of light-hearted com-
ment—jokes about highway robbery, getaway cars leaving a
trail of suds, a legion of police officers combing the roadside for*

discarded empties. The story played like an episode of Dukes of Hazard or Trailer Parks Boys, *with the good ol' boys staying a step ahead of the police.*

What's less funny is that someone else might have been involved in hijacking the tractor-trailer and selling or hiding most of the cargo, and get away with it. If Mr. Haines had accomplices, or was himself an accomplice to a larger criminal enterprise, letting the trail go cold sends entirely the wrong message.

Let's take another kick at the can.

But by all accounts, in spite of the media's and public's interest in bringing others to trial for the crime, police and justice officials appear prepared to let the file be.

THE CARTOONIST

Michael de Adder is a political junkie who couldn't resist the diversions of the Beer Bandit heist. It's his obsession with all things political that lured him during the 1988 federal election from a life of painting (canvasses, not houses) to crafting editorial cartoons. He'd previously dabbled in cartooning for Mount Allison University's student newspaper, *The Argosy*; for eight of the seventeen years since, he's been at it professionally. The signature "de Adder" is seen most regularly on the editorial pages of the Halifax *Daily News* and the Moncton *Times and Transcript*, but also with some frequency in the *National Post*, the Saint John *Telegraph-Journal*, the Ottawa *Hill Times*, and the Ottawa *Citizen*. He's syndicated worldwide through the Artizans group, which is based in Edmonton.

"I don't set out and say what's the political story of the day and I didn't set out to draw three or four or five cartoons on the Beer Bandit story," says thirty-eight-year-old de Adder.

He goes through the news every day looking at headlines that grab him. But he also talks with editors, as he did with Moncton *Times and Transcript* editorial page chief Norbert Cunningham when the Beer Bandit story broke. He talks to people like Cunningham who have their finger on the local pulse to get a sense of whether a given story will resonate with the community. It's not enough for a story to grab just his own attention; it's important for him to determine what's topical at the office "water cooler."

De Adder says the Beer Bandit story was expected to fascinate the public right from the very first headline. In fact, he can't think of any other non-political story with the enduring appeal of the Beer Bandit saga. "It has a life of its own," he says.

The first in de Adder's series of four cartoons showed the image of a Moosehead delivery truck with a masked driver in the cab, chuckling to himself with satisfaction. The overhead caption read: "The Moose Is on the Loose." That was followed by a cartoon showing a Molson Canadian delivery truck accompanied by the caption, "New Brunswickers are so nice. Some guy just volunteered to drive a shipment to Mexico." It's a joke, of course, but given the controversy in 2004, when the New Brunswick government provided assistance for Molson to set up shop in Moosehead's backyard, the last thing Moosehead would want is for Molson to benefit from the kind of free publicity Moosehead was enjoying.

When he heard about the beer-guzzling bears at the backwoods marijuana farm, de Adder couldn't resist. The resulting cartoon shows two bears sharing a case of "El Moosehead" while one remarks that marijuana makes him paranoid.

By the time the trial came around, de Adder was portraying Haines as Dopey from *Snow White and the Seven Dwarfs*, sitting blissfully oblivious in the courtroom. The lawyer before the judge asks, "Your honour, what kind of person could think they could get away with stealing a truckload of beer?"

De Adder may want to consider doing a cartoon about the reappearance of his Beer Bandit cartoons in this book. The story and its cycles may never end.

THE SONGWRITER

When Emmet Bresnahan picked up his copy of the Saint John *Telegraph-Journal* on August 16, 2004, he couldn't put it down.

"I laughed and laughed silently to myself and said: 'Hey, nobody got hurt here, nobody got shot or beaten,'" he says. "I could see Wade Haines going down the Trans-Canada, radio on, during a dark night, saying, 'I've got fifty thousand cans of beer in the back seat, and maybe, just maybe I don't have time to take this where it's supposed to go.'

"Maybe," thought the sixty-three-year-old St. Stephen native, "that's a song!" When the next day's *T-J* headline carried the headline "The Moose Is Loose," he knew he just had to write something.

Bresnahan has been picking at his guitar and "dabbling" at songwriting since 1976; in the past few years, he has been prolific enough to comfortably refer to himself as "a songwriter."

"I write because I feel that I can't let this feeling, this story, this person, this wonder, pass without trying in some way to hold onto it," says Bresnahan. He picks funny subjects for pretty much all of his songs and tucks unorthodox phrasing into every verse. "I have been married for thirty-eight years to the same girl who is my best critic. If she says it's 'so-so,' I know it's a song that is not finished and I give it another lick. I go back at it until she says, 'Yeah, I think that's better.'"

George Gershwin he's not, but he does write funny, catchy lyrics, in a style reminiscent of Stompin' Tom's quirky and popular material. Just as he's not Gershwin, Bresnahan is not Pavarotti, either. But what he lacks in vocal carriage, he makes up for in delivery. His songs are genuinely funny. Here is "The Moose Is Loose," Bresnahan's mid-tempo musical yarn about the Beer Bandit:

Wade Malcolm Haines, age thirty, of no fixed address
Left in a tractor-trailer, number two, headin' west
He had fifty thousand cans of beer, for a depot in TO
Part of a greater shipment, of Moosehead for Mexico

(Chorus)
The Moose is loose, the Moose is loose
It's not on four legs
The Moose is loose, the Moose is loose
It's cans, not kegs
You do the math
You do the math
And keep down your cheers
At eight cans a day, my figures say
A buzz for seventeen years

Two days later, they found the truck
Two hours away in the Falls
The engine was on, the beer was gone,
Sergeant Cameron was called

Cameron said in an interview
A crude operation
Three or four guys, four or five guys
A lack of sophistication

(Chorus)

Wade Malcolm Haines, age 30, now of a fixed address
Said he didn't know
What happened that night
It was all a great big mess

But when he gets out
There's no doubt
A party in that year
And there'll be some drinkin'
And you can be thinkin'
It's Mexican Moosehead beer.

(Chorus)

PART V

A SIXTY-PERCENT CHANCE

THE TEACHER

On his way to work from Fredericton, retired Oromocto High School vice-principal Burton Green used to pass a small cluster of eight, ten, or a dozen kindergarten-age kids boarding their bus, while their mothers watched vigilantly. It always struck him what "precious packages they were"—each one precious in his or her own way. Sixty-five-year-old Green sees the world in such a way that for him, "even Wade Haines is a precious package."

In his thirty-five years as an educator, thirty-two of which were spent at Oromocto High, Green has seen every variety of student come and go: the good, the bad, and the ugly (the latter referring to attitude, not looks, of course). Although he headed the school's mathematics department for a number of years, he was most involved with students' development, and often their problems, during his ten years as vice-principal. During that period, Haines found himself forced to take a seat in Green's office more than a dozen times, discussing his life and his future.

"On one hand, I was startled when I heard about his involvement [with the beer heist], but on the other hand I was not," says Green, adding that "when you're not screwed to the ground," then the unexpected is bound to occur.

Haines was a "sensitive sort of fellow, a kindly sort of fellow," says Green, "not bad" and certainly "not dangerous" in any way. His problems were always the same: recurrent truancy and a failure to apply himself. He was "a cork in the water," just drifting along. "He always had a little grin," says Green, meaning it in a nice way.

Haines was never antagonistic. He never did anything against other students or against the school. "He was just doing things against himself," according to Green.

"He was a pleasant young man to deal with," he adds. "He was never disrespectful with me. Never." That's unlike a lot of students, Green explains, who would sit in Green's office seething with anger, often swearing, sometimes storming out and slamming the door behind them. Although Green hasn't seen Haines in years, he believes "without a doubt that Wade would say he got a fair shake from me and from Oromocto High School."

Green is proud of Oromocto High and its "kids come first" culture, which he attributes to the patience, vision, and leadership of long-time principal David Coughey and Coughey's successor, Jennie Wilson. The latter, says Green, "could see the good in everyone." She had an ability to "reach out to the hurting person." Wilson had a philosophy that caught Green's attention: she didn't just worry about people with low expectations for themselves; she worried more about those who seemed to expect too much of themselves. Even in retirement, Green remains true to this focus on helping youths, as a heavy hitter with Fredericton's Kiwanis organization, whose motto is "Young People Are Priority Number One."

Green believes that there are "benchmarks" in people's lives that set them on one course or another—benchmark events and benchmark people. "Wade didn't seem to have a lot going for him in terms of a support system," says Green. In other words, he had no benchmark people in his life. Green, however, certainly did: he lives just down the street from his ninety-two-year-old father and ninety-four-year-old mother. His father, a Baptist preacher, was a key benchmark in Green's life.

"Where have been the benchmarks for Wade Haines?" he asks, adding that the negative influence throughout most of Haines's life has been drugs. "If they get out there and get into drugs, it gets a hold of their lives and takes them a long way down the wrong road." He admits that having been exposed to drugs for so long, it will be a long, hard challenge for Haines to fight his way back.

Green, however, remains optimistic. "Wade Haines is a precious package, and it would be hoped that somewhere along the line, he would get the support he needs to get him on the right track."

The Believer

George Piers taught school in Fredericton city schools for thirty-four years. He has an undergraduate degree in education, another in math, a master's degree in educational psychology and counselling, and a certificate in advanced studies in psychology. He's a bit frumpy in a stereotypically academic sort of way and he dresses without frills. His focus is on people, not material goods, unless they're being provided to help feed the needy under his care.

"My pick of the lot was grade nines," he explains. "They were a challenge. I also, for seventeen years, had for a homeroom and half days the grade nine kids that nobody wanted—the discipline problems, the drug addicts—because I believe everybody has a possibility of becoming productive in life if they're given a chance.... I've seen many, many of those kids become successful. You know, I still meet them here and there, wherever, and many of them are fine. It's about just getting them on the right track."

Piers is now the administrator of the Fredericton Community Kitchen, after having been a founding member of the service and its facilities twenty-three years ago. He's worked very closely with many people there over the years. When he retired from teaching in the mid 1990s, he was the board president, a post he had held for many years. At the time, he was asked if he'd come up with a job description. He's been in the job ever since, working from a tiny office in the back of the kitchen. "I took it for six months and now it's almost ten years. I thoroughly enjoy it. I enjoy working with the people, I enjoy being able to help people and just seeing progress in people's lives."

Employees, volunteers, and those seeking sustenance all hold Piers in high regard, which is evident in the way they look at him as he wanders from his office to the main dining area. He is the obvious rallying point for the community kitchen.

Piers never taught Wade Haines in school, but he did know his uncle, his grandparents' biological son. "I first met Wade at his uncle's place with his grandparents, when probably Wade was ten or twelve. And Wade surfaced here [at the community kitchen] when he was probably nineteen or twenty."

Haines was in and out of his mother's life, says Piers; his grandparents basically raised him. Piers points out that Haines's mother has had several different live-in partners, one of whom tried to be an authoritarian. This only drove Haines to rebel further.

"Wade found his way here," Piers explains. "I knew who he was, talked to him, chatted with him, that sort of thing. Really it was about three years ago when Wade got out for something. We were sort of having some heart-to-heart talks about truck driving and all the rest of it. Then last spring Wade came back from spending some time at 'Holiday Inn' [i.e., jail] and he did some work for me. He did some carpenter work for me, he dug flower beds, he cleaned out hen pens—I raise exhibition poultry as a hobby out in Kingsclear." Haines told Piers that he appreciated receiving constructive criticism if he didn't do something quite right.

"He wanted to get some help to get his truck driver's licence back, which I did for him. He needed the money and he needed all the rest of it to get that back." Piers says he doesn't know how Haines lost his licence. "I have no idea. I didn't ask those questions. I took him downtown to [the] motor vehicle [department]; we got his licence. He was looking for some jobs. I was actually moving into a new place and so Wade actually stayed there for about six weeks during the course of the summer until he got full-time employment. And he did some work there, like he did some fencing for me, he built some duck coops and helped renovate the henhouse. I got to know Wade pretty well just in the course of conversations, realizing that Wade had two basic addictions, and that of course was alcohol and drugs."

Piers has a bone to pick with trucking companies that don't test their drivers. "To me, it's every bit as bad to be out there on the highway with cocaine in your blood as it is for alcohol."

"I discovered Wade was a person who got discouraged very easily," says Piers. "I think when he was going through these downers is when he did his stupid stuff. And I firmly believe the fact that Wade walked from that truck. I do, because he'd done it twice before. His way of dealing with it [all his problems] was just to get out of it. And of course the girlfriend wasn't any angel. I mean, she's done community hours and time for us here."

Piers alludes to Cari Watson's tendency to enjoy "shopping." "For whatever reason, I don't think she can help herself. So the girlfriend was not any help. Wade has been separate from his own kids for a long time, and her little boy really took to Wade. Caleb really looked at Wade as 'dad,' which he never had. He's probably three or four. And Wade thought the world of him."

Piers believes that pressure from Watson was a major source of stress for Haines. "If he didn't come across with the money, with whatever else, with renting the expensive furniture from the rental place up there, it was like, you know, 'You're not seeing Caleb. You're not doing these things.' That pressure was always there, you know. 'You get out there and get me some money so I can do a little bit of coke here.' All that pressure was there and it was a very difficult relationship which he's been in and out of. And I think that every time he's been in that relationship, he's wound up in jail. You know, if you just look at the pattern from it. To me it was just repeating a pattern."

Piers appeared during the trial and made an offer to the court. "My offer to the court was that I was willing to take Wade into my home, to actually work with Wade during the course of his house arrest, and, you know, we could have these fireside chats that I've done with others before over a course of a time and seen them helped and also getting back into the employment field. I've only had one with me under house arrest, but others I've had with me over the last twelve years—I've been divorced thirteen." Of all those people, no one has ever really tried to take advantage of Piers.

Like Burton Green, Piers is cautiously optimistic about Haines's prospects. "I think Wade has come to the place in his life where he is willing to try to get help to change his life, to fill in the gaps, and move on. I think people, before they can get help, they've got to want it, and I think Wade has done enough jail time, has had enough hard knocks, has been knocked down long enough now, that he wants to get up and move on. I think he's got about a sixty-percent chance of moving on. It depends on all these factors that are out there. It depends on who he gets connected with when he gets out, what he does when he gets out."

Haines has asked Piers if he can stay with him, and Piers has said yes.

Ron "the Cat" Morris agrees with Piers. "This is the longest period of time that Wade's ever been in jail, and I think you're going to see him straighten up. He's got enough time this time that he'll kick whatever problems he has with the drugs and I think he'll be all right, because he's a very intelligent individual. There's all kinds of stuff out there for him."

Even Haines agrees.

"I would say that today I have a sixty-percent chance," he said on June 3, 2005, four sessions into his twenty-six-session drug rehabilitation program. "It depends on how the program goes."

Like anyone in an addiction program, he needs to learn how to recognize the triggers that put him in the risk zone. A lot of it has to do with people he periodically ends up with. "These people I was hanging out with are not my friends," he says. "They're just the people you go to see when you're doing that type of thing"—meaning, obviously, the drugs.

Haines is highly conscious—when not in his diminished capacity—of what's what, who's who, and who he can be if the cards come up right.

During his time in jail, Haines began attending church services. Piers is surprised by this, but he thinks it is a good sign. "He was telling me that when he gets out he wants to continue with that. He's got this broad range from the Catholic to the Pentecostal and he's sort of leaning towards the Pentecostal end of it, and he said for once in his life he'd like to be able to find a girlfriend, maybe eventually a wife who is not in the drugs, who's not, well, almost a street person, because that apparently is what he's been dealing with. But I do see good potential in him because Wade is a good worker. He's not scared to work."

According to Piers that is a necessary characteristic for anyone who wants to straighten out. The other necessary characteristics include "determination and the desire to [straighten out]. And right now, I think he's got the whole works of it."

Haines admits that he is at a crossroads and that religion is helping him choose the right path. "I can take my life down the high road or the low road," he says. "I've got to keep my faith in God and Christ."

But wait a minute, you might say, don't a lot of criminals use that line? Of course they do, but it's normally an ace they play while seeking leniency or early parole. Haines needs neither: he's been convicted, he's served his time, and he's been released.

"I'm not religious," he adds, "but I am a Christian. That's what gets me through every day. I have to have faith to get through this."

A standard day in jail demands faith. In the Saint John facility, recreation is very minimal. Inmates get fifteen to twenty minutes per day outside and if it's raining, there's no outside access. To pass the time, apart from thinking about God and Christ, Haines read books by Clive Cussler, John Grisham, and Dean Toombs.

Piers allowed Haines to call him collect at his home at least once or twice a week, usually for about twenty minutes at a time, but sometimes up to an hour and a half.

"A couple of times he was pretty depressed," says Piers. "He was almost to the point where, if he could have put something around his neck and hung by it, he would have done it, and I was really concerned about him."

Piers's assessment of a forty-percent chance of failure is based on experience. "I firmly believe he has a better chance of succeeding rather than failing. Now, as far as ever driving transport truck again, that's highly doubtful, but you know, there's gravel trucks, there's other types of trucks, there's short-haul trucks around here, non-perishable stuff."

As for Haines's refusal to identify the others involved in the beer heist, Piers looks at the circumstances practically. "There is the possibility that Wade may feel that it's better to be alive and on the inside than squealing and saying what actually really happened and being dead on the outside."

Piers says Haines's best quality is his personality. "Wade has a terrific personality. He has terrific work ethics, and right now he has determination and a desire to change, so I think those are the qualities that he's showing right now.... I think there's a good sixty-percent chance that Wade is going to succeed."

THE MOTHER

"I'm his mother. I love him with all my heart. But I don't always like what Wade does, the choices he makes."

Theresa (Terri) Reid has opened her heart and her mind for the purposes of an interview. It seems therapeutic, almost cathartic for the fifty-four-year-old Fredericton-area woman to do so. No other forum has provided such an outlet for Reid, whose ongoing problems with a troublesome child reached their nadir on Thursday, August 19, 2004, when she learned that it was her son's tractor-trailer that had gone missing and was receiving so much media attention. Since then, her life has been topsy-turvy, and her work as senior human resources advisor to the New Brunswick Department of Supply and Services has been difficult. The department employs three hundred and fifty people, and Reid's work includes obligations to several pan-provincial committees that deal with HR issues throughout the New Brunswick civil service. She's been in the provincial bureaucracy for nearly thirty years.

She went to teacher's college in Fredericton from 1970 to 1972, when she was married to Wade's natural father. Nine months later, Wade was born. She received her certificate in human resource management from the University of New Brunswick and has been certified by the International Personnel Management Association (IPMA), which means she can work in HR pretty much anywhere in the world.

Two weeks before he went missing, Haines had gone to his mother's house with his Brenway tractor. He'd come to pick up some second-hand Tommy Hilfiger and other brand-name clothes that Terri had purchased at Frenchy's.

"He had come out to pick up some stuff," she explains, "and he was talking and he said he had a load, I think it was peat moss. But he said, 'Sometimes I haul big loads of alcohol, liquor and stuff, and it's worth quite a bit.' And he said, 'I'm so proud of that. People trust me, and mom, you know I would never do anything to an employer. I've always been really good with that.' We were just talking. I have no idea why that would come up, but I really guess deep in my heart I believe Wade didn't do it, exactly what he was accused of and charged with. What he did do I have no idea. The following week I didn't hear from him."

That week she was on vacation, and like everyone else in North America she heard about the missing truck and its novel contents through the media. "I didn't pay a bit of attention to it," she says. "It never clicked one little bit until that Thursday morning we were at the lake. We got a knock on our door at the trailer at about eight o'clock in the morning and it was the park manager. He said, 'Terri, was that Wade that had that truck?' And I said, 'What do you mean, Peter?'" He told Reid he was pretty sure he'd heard Wade's name mentioned on the CBC.

"Well, I just fell apart. I didn't know what to do," says Reid. "I was going into Hampton that morning to go to 'Curves' to exercise and when I was in Hampton I picked up a paper and read it and there it was. I went to the RCMP station in Hampton and told them who I was, and at this point he was just missing. And as his mother I was devastated, I mean just horrified. I really, honestly, truly never dreamt that he would do something like that. He's done things before and been in lots of trouble but actually doing that...."

She says that Sgt. John Welsher of the Hampton detachment helped her a lot. "I thought [Wade] was dead. I was a total and complete shambles trying to think that no news was good news.... It wasn't until the next week that Sgt. Welsher called me and told me they'd found Wade. I was relieved that he was alive, but then I said, 'Well I'm glad he's alive, now I'm going to kill him.'"

Reid says that driving truck was the only job that Haines had ever felt truly happy about. She says he would never have done anything to jeopardize that as long as he was thinking straight.

Reid has spent a considerable amount of time at the doctor since August of 2004. She's on medication to try to keep things level. She's gained thirty pounds. The hardest part is that she can't escape the story. "Every time you'd turn around it would be on the news, in the paper."

Reid has had little if any contact with Haines since the affair began. "I'm scared to see him because when he was younger he was in Kingsclear [a Fredericton-area adult correctional facility], and to see him like that in that place just about killed me." When he was prison, she sent him a little money, wrote the odd letter, and made the occasional phone call, but because of the pain she avoided seeing him.

The pain is that much worse, thanks to her professional, in-depth understanding of people and how they deal with issues in their lives. It's horribly ironic that one of her primary interests at work overlaps with the types of issues facing Haines.

"I'm trying to see where he's going," she explains. "I'm doing a two-year certificate program in choice theory, reality therapy, and lead-management from the William Glasser Institute. These are professional applications that are used in some of the schools with teaching." She's actually doing her advanced practicum in this area of study.

Glasser is famous for his writings and theories in human behaviour. "Good or bad, everything we do is our best choice at that moment," he wrote. Choice theory suggests that all we do is behave, that almost all behaviour is chosen, and that we are driven by our genes to satisfy five basic needs. According to Glasser's theories, people are more likely to encounter trouble when they're not meeting their five basic needs in life: survival (including nourishment, shelter, and sex), power (which includes achievement and feeling worthwhile), freedom (which includes independence), fun (which is self-explanatory), and what Glasser calls the most important of the five: love and belonging. Of those five, Reid believes Haines is most missing his power, his achievement.

"It all focuses on when you make choices," she explains, "and I've written Wade about that and I said, 'What do you want out of life?' and 'What are you doing to get that?' and 'Is it working, and if not, what's your plan going to be to make it work?'"

As part of her talking to Haines about choice theory and its related counselling techniques, Reid prompted him to take classes and courses while at Westmoreland, such as the drug program, "which is great," she says. There's never been a previous program that he's stayed in.

"When he was in Saint John a year or a year and a half ago," she recalls, "they let him out into a halfway house for the last couple of weeks or so, and he was supposed to go to counselling, and he always had a reason not to go. He had a sore shoulder or he had a sore leg or he had a cold, and they ended up, two days before he was being released, taking him back to Old Black River Road [location of the Saint John Regional Correctional Centre]. He just wouldn't face that he has a problem. It took *me* a long time to face that he had a problem."

Reid says that Haines seemed to believe throughout the Beer Bandit trial that he was going to be proven innocent. "I don't know if he's got a total perception of what happened," she explains. "He wrote and I've got a card which I don't think I've thrown away—a Christmas card—that said, 'From the Beer Bandit.' I just thought it was a joke, that he didn't really mean it. I think he was just trying to be a little light-hearted about it, but he said something like, 'I'll see you next Christmas,' because he's spent the last couple of Christmases in jail. He spent his thirtieth birthday in jail. He spent his thirty-first birthday in jail." One is the same as the other because Wade Haines was born on Christmas Eve. "For me that's just absolutely devastating," says Reid.

Her work in human resource management gives her a perspective on human activity that most mothers of criminals don't have, unless they set about to study it. But even so, she's at a loss to explain the root of Haines's problems. "I don't know where it went wrong. He was the best kid. We had report cards from his Grade One teacher saying he was such a delight to have in his class, that he was absolutely wonderful, but somewhere along the early teenage years he started going with the wrong crowd. Something happened to him."

Haines is not lacking in natural abilities, insists Reid. "He's very bright. He can be very articulate when he wants to be. In fact, when he was in Kingsclear he did the GED program in three weeks, wrote his exam, and passed everything."

She says truancy was a constant problem for Haines. "They couldn't keep him in school. In high school, he just wouldn't stay. He was kicked out all the time. I went before the school board trying to get him back in.... He just wouldn't go. He just wasn't motivated."

In addition to the truancy, there were also the drugs, which led Haines to make many bad decisions. Reid remembers one particularly unpleasant episode from the days when Haines was living with her parents, Alan and Doris Maunder. "He was really close to my dad for a long time. But it was then, when he was younger, that he must have started getting into the dope, using money that he would steal from my dad. He stole all kinds of things out of the shed, would sell them, like chain saws and this and that. It killed my dad, not literally, but it broke his heart like this whole thing is breaking mine. He actually stole money out of my dad's bank account. He wrote cheques on it.... It devastated dad because he was his only grandchild. That just hurt my dad so bad."

Reid says Haines never really explained why he stole from his grandfather. "I tried at one time [to get an explanation from him] when he was living with us. I asked what was wrong that had happened. He would tell me nothing but that he loved his grandfather very much."

Asked whether Haines and his grandfather ever reconciled, Reid says, "Yes, I think so, in their own way. But when dad passed away, the will was divided three ways: my brother, myself, and Wade—forty, forty, twenty. Wade got twenty percent of the inheritance, which wasn't much. It was less than $15,000, but it was gone," she snaps her fingers, "just like that. It would have gone right down into dope or whatever. I think he just got into the dope, got into the wrong crowd." One member of that crowd would be Cari Watson, whom Reid, like many others, sees as a negative influence on Haines.

On a more positive note, Reid has fond memories of camping with her son. When he was twenty-nine, he spent a couple of summer weekends staying in a tent pitched near Reid's trailer, and they went to local barn dances at Lake Maguaguadavic. "He would carry my little cooler up there and take care of me and carry it home for me, and we had a great time. It was probably one of the nicest times I've had with him as an adult."

To the question of whether Haines will be spending any time at the Reid household when he's released, the answer is a flat no, which corresponds with Haines's opinion that at thirty-one, he has no business living in his mother's home.

"I want him to be independent," she explains. "When he was about twelve, thirteen, somewhere along there, he was having a problem going to school and we took him to a counsellor and he did some evaluations and he told us Wade would be in his thirties before he grew up." With Haines now in his thirties, Reid hopes the counsellor's prediction will come true.

After all is said and done, Reid has not abandoned Haines. "I think that deep down he's got a lot of good. He's had the right values instilled in him at a young age. He went to Sunday school, he went to scouts, he was very polite and mannerly and shy as a young boy. I believe he'd kind and generous when he can be. When he has something to share, he would share it with, I think, anybody. I just think he got in with the wrong crowd and I mean the really big-time wrong crowd."

Reid is hopeful but not naïve about Haines's prospects for positive change. His work ethic is a tremendous help, she says, and so is his connection with George Piers. Reid is proud of having passed on a strong work ethic to her son, although, somewhat paradoxically, she sees that same work ethic as one of her shortcomings. "I've always had to work," she says, "and I guess I came from the old philosophy that dad instilled in me—your work always comes first. And if I have one failing thing as a mother I think that's what I did wrong, was working too much and not paying enough attention. My dad always worked a lot and hard. Your work came first and family came second. Well, everything has totally changed now and I'm a great advocate for young people—you need time to go be with your family."

Asked whether Haines's elongated fifteen minutes of fame will make it harder or easier for him to find his way, Reid has no doubt that things will be harder. "I think it'll make it harder because people aren't going to forget and he's going to have to live it down a lot." She says it's going to pop up everywhere he goes. "The Department of the Environment had a Chinese auction last Christmas for the United Way. I went up to buy some tickets and they had one of the [Moosehead Beer Bandit] promotional T-shirts on the table. One of the staff was behind me and she had to literally catch me. I pretty near fainted. It just broke my heart to see that there." Reid thinks the ubiquity of the Beer Bandit craze will have a similarly negative effect on Haines himself.

As for Reid, she says her friends and coworkers have been wonderful. "Even with my course and that, the facilitators know and it's like, 'He's an adult and he makes his own choices in life.' I did one of my [course] papers on him when he was in Saint John [Regional Correctional Centre] the first time. I had to do a presentation, just three or four pages, on how I was using choice theory in my own life. Reid wrote about talking with her son and being proud of him for turning his life around: he'd gotten out of jail and quickly found a job. Sadly, though, Haines's success was short-lived. "It fell through," says his mother. "It didn't last."

THE FORMER BEER BANDIT

After his conviction for the Beer Bandit heist Haines was sent first to the Saint John Regional Correctional Centre, and then to the Westmoreland Corrections Canada Minimum Security Institution. The institution is located high on a hill halfway between Moncton and the New Brunswick–Nova Scotia border, overlooking the village of Dorchester, the pastoral Memramcook Valley, and, in the near distance, the majestic Bay of Fundy. It's strange that such awesome panoramic vistas are best viewed from a criminal kibbutz. On the less scenic side, at certain times of day, modern Westmoreland stands in the shadows of the eerily Gothic Dorchester Penitentiary, the one-time maximum-security fright house of Atlantic Canada, where the worst of the worst criminals were locked up.

The infamous Dorchester was built in the nineteenth century in the style of the seventeenth-century French architect François Mansart. Westmoreland, by contrast, is a modern complex, consisting of a school, communal housing that resembles a cluster of urban townhouses, common areas, a baseball diamond surrounded by an oval track, and a sizeable working farm. It houses all types of convicts, from white-collar criminals to violent offenders, who have exhibited consistently exemplary behaviour while serving their time in higher-level institutions. The Westmoreland institution is designed to integrate people back into society. The security level is so low that, theoretically, an inmate could just walk away from Westmoreland. But they're there because it's believed they won't. They're there to clean the slate.

For one of our interviews, Haines arrived from working a tractor and a dusty combine. It was obvious from his enthusiasm that the tractor reminded him of the freedom of trucking, shifting gears, and being "free," so to speak, in the outdoors. The Saint John Regional Correctional Centre nearly drove him around the bend with its meaningless, do-nothing sensory deprivation—no television, no radio, no access to computers.

Unlike the Saint John correctional facility, Westmoreland gives its inmates things to do. Haines's mornings there were spent attending sessions of the moderate-intensity National Substance Abuse Program (NSAP). Haines was placed in the moderate-intensity program because he was a periodic user—"I only binged," he says—whereas a high-intensity user would have been stoned pretty much all the time, requiring a much more rigorous program. There were ten men in the spring 2005 NSAP program Haines attended. They found themselves there after induction training, which teaches new inmates how to avoid certain types of people and activities "on the inside"—people who thrive on continuing drug use and all its related problems. Watching who you associate with is just as important on the inside as it is when you get back to the outside.

Afternoons at Westmoreland involve farm or related work around the institution. Evenings are reserved for baseball or walking loops around the oval track. The work, like the freedom of the tractor and the combine, goes on seven days a week.

Haines makes all the usual jokes about "club fed." In all honesty, aspects of Westmoreland aren't exactly horrible—although people aren't lining up to be let in, either. During his time there, Haines resided in a "house" accommodating six to eight men. They bunked in pairs, shared shopping, cooking, and cleaning duties, and watched television. They had access to computers but not to the internet. The guys in Haines's house were, he says, a pretty good group of guys—mostly family men who just wanted to serve their time and return home.

On Wednesday, July 20, 2005, Haines was released from Westmoreland into the custody of a Fredericton halfway house. A week later, getting used to the fact that he could suddenly use the telephone, go on-line, or walk into a Tim Horton's, he declared that one of his priorities is to watch not only what he does, but also what he says. He has no desire, for example, to speak to the media, except for the interviews conducted for this book, which were based on trust. Talking, he realizes, has gotten him into enough trouble.

He immediately began volunteering at the Fredericton Community Kitchen—cooking, cleaning, and performing general kitchen duties—with "believer" George Piers at the helm and at his side. After the two-week volunteer stint, the John Howard Society came forward with a twelve-week work program, which put Haines in the kitchen's formal employ.

For the first time in memory, he feels he has a clear head. There's no grass, no alcohol, and no cocaine pulsing through his veins. "It's great to be out and to be drug-free," he says. "Everything is clear."

Piers says that he can see a clarity in Haines that he has not seen for quite some time. "He's not looking like somebody just hit him with a two-by-four," Piers laughs. And Haines is demonstrating a very positive attitude, the likes of which Piers has not seen in him before. "Succeed today and move on to tomorrow" is how the mentor sees it. "And you've got to be realistic. There are going to be up days and there are going to be down days. You've got to build yourself an emotional support system," some of which can be found at the community kitchen.

According to Haines, everyone he has encountered at the community kitchen has been supportive.

Haines says he is doing many things to help avoid recidivism: making amends to people he's hurt, absorbing the encouragement of supporters, and, most important of all, trying to disprove the

RCMP report that was filed as a matter of standard procedure when he first applied for parole. The report opined that it was not a question of "if" Haines would commit another crime and find himself back in prison, but simply "when." "I think of that every day," says Haines.

He found his exposure before the general public "degrading and humiliating." Strangely, however, Haines feels that people were so caught up in the novelty and humour of the story that they spent less time focusing on him as an individual. The latter, he admits, is his job, his responsibility.

No matter what else Haines might have been guilty of, being irresponsible, he readily admits, was foremost on the list. That said, he still swears that he did not steal the beer. He says he believes that the authorities kept him in jail after returning to New Brunswick "partly for my own safety."

As for the beer, "I'm still curious as to who took it," he says, although he claims to have some theories.

During one early interview, he pointed to his cooperative attitude toward the police as evidence of his innocence. He waited in Lindsay, knowing that the New Brunswick–based Mounties were on their way. He voluntarily went to the local police headquarters for his interview and interrogation. There were no handcuffs or shackles used to restrain him. Because of the summer heat, both back windows were down in the RCMP cruiser during the long drive back to New Brunswick. He admits that when you're in that kind of situation, escaping is one of the unavoidable thoughts that run through your head. He didn't try to escape, of course, any more than he tried to walk away from Westmoreland, an act that would set an inmate's life back hopelessly.

After first being arrested and experiencing that journey in the back of the RCMP cruiser from Lindsay to Fredericton, he says he thought about how he would turn his life around. "I really felt at the time, on the way back from Ontario, 'when I get back there..."'

The "back there" that Haines had in mind went on hold for quite some time. There's been the trial, stints in two jails, the soul-searching process of drug rehabilitation, and the experience of relentless public humiliation.

Haines's "back there" will be one of two possible scenarios: recidivism or a serious change in his life. George Piers prefers to believe in the latter. "I'm seeing the ending that Wade is going to go into community college, retrain for something other than truck driving, which is his first love, be successful at it, find somebody that is compatible, who is a strong personality, marry, settle down, and so-called live happily ever after. But there are going to be a lot of rough points between now and then."

Haines says he'll take things one day at a time, with a clear head, intent on proving the RCMP report wrong.